MW00364242

Winter Music

Winter

Music

COMPOSING THE NORTH

JOHN LUTHER ADAMS

Foreword by Kyle Gann

WESLEYAN UNIVERSITY PRESS

Middletown, Connecticut

Wesleyan University Press
Middletown, CT 06459
www.wesleyan.edu/wespress

© 2004 by John Luther Adams
All music illustrations © Taiga Press (BMI)
All rights reserved

Printed in the United States of America 5 4 3
ISBN 978-0-8195-6742-0

Wesleyan University Press is a member of the Green
Press Initiative. The paper used in this book meets their
minimum requirement for recycled paper.

Library of Congress Cataloging-in-Publication Data
Adams, John Luther, 1953–
Winter music : composing the North /
John Luther Adams; foreword by Kyle Gann.
    p.   cm.
Includes bibliographical references (p.   ),
discography (p.   ), and index.
ISBN 0-8195-6742-6 (hardcover : alk. paper)
1. Music. 2. Composition (Music). 3. Alaska—
Description and travel. I. Title.
ML60.A25   2004
780′.92—dc22   2004009749

. . . to the North . . .

May it always be a geography of hope.

Contents

Illustrations

Foreword

by Kyle Gann

JOHN LUTHER ADAMS:

MUSIC AS A GEOGRAPHY OF THE SPIRITUAL

John Luther Adams is such an optimist. "The places we live in resonate within us," he writes in one of the first of these essays. "The sounds around us . . . all echo in the music of a place."

Of course, John can say that: He lives in Alaska. He wanders across miles of frozen tundra, climbs mountains to see the vista of the Arctic Ocean on the other side, loses any sense of time watching the sun move parallel to the horizon, and has encounters with grizzly bears. A place can resonate in your music when it's an amazing place. He's like Mahler in this respect, who composed in the Alps and who, when a visitor admired the view from his window, said, "You needn't stand staring at that—I've already composed it all." Or even like Chopin, whose good luck, Schoenberg claimed, was that any time he wanted to do something that had never been done before, needed simply to write in F♯ major. There's an advantage in being first, and, in a way, John is simply the first to compose the great expanses of white in the Alaskan wilderness.

But Adams's statement does not solely refer to Alaska: it claims to speak for us all. What of composers who live in Union City, New Jersey; Cincinnati, Ohio; La Jolla, California? How are those places supposed to echo in their music? Normally one dismisses such questions without thinking about them, but once Adams has brought them up, they have an irritating habit of sticking. I've listened to Adams's music for many years and loved it, but reading his words, I have thoughts I've never had before. What does

Red Hook, New York, have to do with my music? Is the Hudson Valley having some subconscious effect that I'm unaware of? A lot of composers live in the Hudson Valley; will some future historian find among us synchronicities that unite us stylistically? Do the spacing of the small towns, the rolling hills before the visible abrupt rise of the Catskills, the very unidirectionality of the river itself, find echoes in my work?

And let's turn it around: should the artist be careful about where he lives, choosing his resonances carefully? After all, Adams didn't just get transferred to Alaska, he moved there by choice and has doggedly remained there, despite career disadvantages that attend living in geographical isolation. Nietszche, in a dissenting view, claimed that genius needed a warm climate — but at least he agreed that geography has a crucial effect. Should the artist seek wilderness, cultural life, or simply a climate and landscape congenial to him?

Or should the artist, living where he or she must, contribute to making his own landscape more livable? Adams sanctifies Alaska in his music; can each of us do the same to the place where we live? We live in a society in which little attention is given to the sonic aspect of the human environment. Is it the artist's job to be a caretaker of the environment, possibly by revealing it, making it more evident to the people who live there and who would otherwise casually ignore it? One thinks of the archetypal environment-listening piece, John Cage's 4'33", which was premièred, after all, in a specific place — not Carnegie Hall, nor some downtown loft, but a little outdoor theater in the woods outside Woodstock, New York. Commitment to chance notwithstanding, Cage certainly picked a lovely, natural environment to listen to.

These are the kinds of unfamiliar, uneasy, yet strangely attractive thoughts that the music and writings of John Luther Adams inspire. He writes evocatively about Alaska, but not so much in a way to make you want to go there as to make you question your relation to your own environment. In our sophisticated, technological, rationalist, secular world, we dismiss as superstition the idea of any necessary connection between musical expression and geography. Adams tells us: not so fast. Music doesn't come entirely from the rational mind, after all, but partly from the animal, spirit part of us that is strangely affected by sacred spaces.

One thing I can tell you about the Hudson River: everyone knows that that river runs straight down to New York City, and here we're all sonically aware of the *absence* of the great noise of Manhattan. (We even queasily remember that the 9/11 hijackers used this river as their guide to steer toward the World Trade Center.) Adams is far away from such daily reminders of urban civilization, but when he refers to himself as an "out-of-town composer," the town he has in mind is New York. Yet he draws a distinction between the *regional* and the *provincial* that might not have been possible a few generations ago. Thanks to the internet and the gradual decentralization of society, the regional artist need no longer be assumed provincial. While Adams may be one of the most self-consciously regional of musicians, his music need not be judged for that reason by a less sophisticated standard.

Let's also not overstate Adams's isolation—I see him in Manhattan as much as I do almost anyone. For several years he was president of the American Music Center in New York: not at American music's periphery, but at its center. For all that his home lies thousands of miles away from musical centers of activity, he is not an *aesthetically* isolated figure, but remains conversant with the aesthetic concerns of his contemporaries, and heir to some of American music's central traditions.

First of all, as a youth Adams encountered a book which has been a formative influence on several generations of American composers, from Cage and Nancarrow and Harrison to Larry Polansky and Mikel Rouse: Henry Cowell's *New Musical Resources*, written in 1917–19 and first published in 1930. The most revolutionary part of the book was a chapter outlining a new approach to rhythm drawn from analogies with pitch. Cowell chafed at the rhythmic limitations of European tradition, based as it is on groupings of only two or three or four beats. Why not five, asked Cowell, or seven, or thirteen? Why not several tempos going at the same time? Several meters at once? Repeating rhythms of different lengths all going at once?

This is one of the ideas that takes off in Adams's music. Just as Conlon Nancarrow, reclusive writer of rhythmically complex music for player pianos, kept charts from Cowell's book on his studio wall all his life, Adams too has spent his life exploring ideas expressed in Cowell's book. In a piece like *Clouds of Forgetting, Clouds of Unknowing*, the celesta will play nine even notes per measure while the piano plays seven and the vibraphone five. In *Dream in White on White*, the solo violins will repeat five-beat phrases against the four-beat phrases of the viola and cello. On a much larger level, the string orchestra chords of *In the White Silence* articulate a slow, steady pulse against the dissimilar pulses of the other players.

Another source for Adams's aesthetic is the late Morton Feldman. In an era of music that exploited maximum variety, Feldman created a world with a single marked dynamic—"as soft as possible"—and one made from reiterative lines almost devoid of attack or articulation. In a world of twenty-minute pieces, Feldman wrote monochrome pieces of three, four, six hours without a break. The main thing that Adams inherited from Feldman was the permission to limit his materials, to give the listener unarticulated color with little surface detail to hang on to.

However, while Feldman's monochromaticism remained locked in a dissonant, tonality-negating modernist vocabulary, Adams latched onto white as a pervasive metaphor. The number of Adams pieces, including some of his longest, that contain only the "white" notes of the keyboard, without a single sharp or flat, is rather astounding: *In the White Silence, In a Treeless Place, Only Snow, Dream in White on White, The Farthest Place*, four of the

Five Yup'ik Dances, and much of the *Five Athabascan Dances*. Likewise, while Adams has not yet rivaled the six-hour length of Feldman's Second String Quartet (I have a hunch he will some day), he has written longer orchestra pieces than Feldman's forty-five-minute magnum opus *For Samuel Beckett*. *Clouds of Forgetting, Clouds of Unknowing* is a sixty-minute continuum, *In the White Silence* seventy-five minutes.

Cowell's rhythmic complexity plus Feldman's monochromaticism: this is the standard thumbnail description of Adams's music. In itself, it does not greatly distinguish him from a number of other composers who live in New York, Los Angeles, San Francisco, and Seattle. In fact, Adams fits neatly into what I consider the two primary movements in early twenty-first-century American music, postminimalism and totalism. Like the postminimalists (William Duckworth, Janice Giteck, Daniel Lentz, Elodie Lauten, Paul Dresher, and many others), Adams has returned to tonality in a nontraditional, unsentimental way. There is no nostalgia here, there are no "chord progressions," no references to "great music of the past." The seven-tone scale is recreated anew in all its innocence, freed to create color fields, no longer burdened by the syntax of the tonal "language."

Like the totalists (Rhys Chatham, Mikel Rouse, Art Jarvinen, Michael Gordon, Ben Neill, myself) Adams is fascinated by pulses at different tempos. His music is almost always composed in layers, and those layers move at different speeds, from the rapid to the glacial. Many composers born in the 1950s have been educated by Cowell, inspired by Feldman and Nancarrow, given a new starting point by the minimalism of Steve Reich and Philip Glass. Adams is right in there, and in good company. When he says, in "Strange and Sacred Noise," "I want my music to have both formal rigor and visceral impact"—this is virtually the totalist credo, the credo of an entire generation of American composers weary of the sterile abstractions of the avant-garde music they studied in college.

So this formulation links Adams with his generation; it is our job to clarify why he stands out. To Cowell's rhythmic theories and Feldman's monochromaticism we must add: Alaska. After all, totalism is mostly a New York–based, rock 'n' roll–inspired movement. The musics of Chatham, Rouse, Gordon pound away with the energy of electric guitars. Adams's music doesn't. Those rhythmic complexities are there, but rather than pound, they shimmer. His percussion music can be explosive, but its energy is more closely related to Inuit drumming or the elemental force of ice breaking up on a great river. Although Adams came of age playing rock, he is no rocker wannabe. This is not the virtuoso complexity of *homo technologicus*, but the subtle and impassive complexity of nature. We're not meant to completely understand what we're hearing. And unlike the postminimalists, Adams sometimes—as in *Clouds of Forgetting*—unleashes the whole chromatic scale on us. Postminimalism is a movement of clarity and human scale; totalism is an urban music of hard edges. Adams's model is nature, his method a quiet focuslessness, and his sense of scale is vast.

Of all the words I could use to describe Adams' music—beautiful, shimmering, vast, luminous, ecstatic—the only one that might be taken as negative in its connotations is "impersonal." Even his abundant melodies are never bouncy or ornamented or circuitous or eccentric, but stately, gradual in their rhythms, choosing their pitches without regard to harmony or surprise. But impersonality of this type is no deficiency; Notre Dame Cathedral is similarly impersonal, the Mojave Desert is impersonal, Uluru rock in Australia is impersonal, the Aurora Borealis is impersonal. Adams writes his music impersonal because he trusts the material and considers sound itself more interesting than his own idiosyncrasies of character. Like the Box Drum Dance he describes in "Winter Music," his music is ritual—not self-expression. The totalist credo I quote above is followed with the words: "Through the discipline of an overall formal symmetry, I hope to move beyond self-expression and the limits of my own imagination to a deeper awareness of the sound itself . . . I'm most deeply moved when the music has little or nothing to do with personal expression."

This is perhaps the area in which Adams most separates himself off from most of the composers of his generation. Art as self-expression was a product of arts education of the 1950s and 1960s: "paint what you feel," children were told. But an ancient tradition, expounded by (among others) Ananda K. Coomaraswamy in *The Christian and Oriental Philosophy of Art*—a book that Cage pointed to as an influence—says that in true art, self-expression may be an inevitable side effect, but should never be a goal. Or, as Charles Ives writes in *Essays before a Sonata*, "The nearer we get to the mere expression of emotion, . . . the further we get away from art." What art should express, as Adams puts it, is "the larger fabric of life—the life of the individual, the life of the community, the life of the land and the life of the animals and spirits that inhabit this place."

Similarly, Adams's writing is impersonal in an interestingly analogous way. I can assure you it sounds just like him, and his personality comes across on the page just as it does in the flesh. He is not fascinated by himself, he never details the vicissitudes of his career, he reveals no personal anguish, he doesn't use his writing to settle old scores like so many artists (well, except maybe with the professor who wanted him to write a bassoon sonata—an uncharacteristically revealing vignette). He writes about the birds that still chirp in 55-below weather, about the stone rings that reveal the presence of ancient man, about the brightness of the Aurora Borealis. In the strict Jungian sense, and as befits an Aquarian, John has an extroverted sensibility: he is more moved by the things that go on outside him than by the things that go on inside him, or at least more apt to talk about them.

One of the things he talks most about is painting. Very few composers bring up the subject of painting with such regularity

—Feldman being the obvious exception—and while Adams's divagations on music history are a little distant and theoretical, his relationship to painting is immediate, unselfconscious, and affectionate. Reversing the nineteenth-century flow of inspiration, his music aspires to the condition of painting, and you frequently feel he would love to reduce it to simply color and space. "[T]he feeling of endless space is exhilarating," he writes in "Winter Music." "This is what I want to find in music!"

Ultimately, Alaska and complex rhythms aside, Adams's music is most of all a yearning for transcendence, for which his obsession with color and light are a musician's visual metaphors. This yearning pervades his texts. You get the feeling, not that he discovered transcendence in Alaska, but that he went there in search of it. In ". . . the lines disappear completely . . . ," a friend notices the middle section of Adams's work *The Far Country of Sleep* where "nothing happens," and says, "That's what you really want to do, isn't it?" In recent years Adams's music has moved not only away from self-expression but from musical rhetoric itself toward pure background reinterpreted as foreground, toward the "soundless sound" of Zen meditation, awareness without differentiation. Narrative is too limiting, not truthful enough: "instead of the arc of a story," he writes, "I want the music to have the more objective presence of a place" ("Roots and Influences"). The story he tells of the two paintings, one of which was ruined by having an object in the foreground from which you could get your bearings? That's a clue about listening to Adams's music.

And so we need to add one more term to our formulation: John Luther Adams equals Cowell's rhythms plus Feldman's unarticulated color fields, plus Alaska, plus a sense of spirituality that yearns for the obliteration of self, and a return to the world spirit. Adams is rare among recent American musical figures (parallel to Arvo Pärt in Europe) in his willingness to talk about spirituality, to make that rather than any technical desiderata the focus of any discussion of his own music. Being a music theory writer myself,

I have here described his music in technical terms, but he avoids them. Considered in terms of Ives's famous distinction between substance and manner, Adams prefers to speak only of substance, defined by Ives in *Essays before a Sonata* as "the body of a conviction which has its birth in the spiritual consciousness, whose youth is nourished in the moral consciousness, and whose maturity as a result of all this growth is then represented in a mental image. This is appreciated by the intuition. . . . So it seems that "substance" is too indefinite to analyze, in more specific terms. It is practically indescribable. Intuitions (artistic or not?) will sense it—process, unknown. Perhaps it is an unexplained consciousness of being nearer God, or being nearer the devil—of approaching truth or approaching unreality—a silent something felt in the truth-of-nature in Turner against the truth-of-art in Botticelli."

That the truth-of-nature in Adams is so different from the truth-of-nature in Ives may be largely due to the differences between New England and Alaska.

So let this serve to define John Luther Adams musically for now—surely anyone who reads these pages has already listened to his ravishing music, or will be inspired to do so shortly. In addition to his musical attributes, there are personal characteristics that will become evident: the kindness and gentleness of a Lou Harrison, a sly sense of humor comparable to Cage's, an earnestness and a refusal to stoop to negativity that are nearly without parallel in professional circles. The sincerity that imbues Adams's music pervades the pages of this book as well—not the sincerity of a naïf, but that of an idealist who knows all too well how the world works, but believes that something worthwhile is achieved only by moving toward higher ground, toward the light that draws us on.

Red Hook, New York
March 2004

Preface

Barnett Newman observed that an artist sometimes writes to have something to read. I think I know what he meant.

I'm a composer. So when I write, it's usually about music. I write to articulate for myself my own evolving understanding of my work. I also write to invite listeners into the musical landscapes of specific works, or to suggest the broader context from which the music grows.

Music is an inseparable part of the fabric of my life. So in addition to essays about music, these writings include excerpts from journals and anecdotes from travel, work, and daily life. I hope they will speak not only to fellow musicians and artists, but also to other readers who share my aspiration to live creatively in turbulent times.

In a world with more than six billion of us human animals, we can no longer hold ourselves apart from what we simplistically call "nature." Nature encompasses our entire world. It is the original source of human life and creativity. For me, nature and music are one and the same.

Music is not what I do. Music is how I live. It's not how I express myself. It's how I understand the world.

Through countless centuries indigenous people have listened to the voices of the North. For those of us who have lost our deepest connections with place, their knowledge is essential. Patiently and gently, my friends and collaborators Adeline Peter Raboff, James Nageak, Lincoln Tritt, and Doreen Simmonds have instructed me in the rich nuances of their native cultures, showing me how to live here not as a visitor, but as an inhabitant of this place.

Before I first came to Alaska, I read the poems and essays of John Haines. John's vision of the North has inspired my own. For almost twenty-five years now, he has been a supportive colleague and an affectionate friend.

The writings of Barry Lopez have had a profound influence on my work. Barry has said that he and I are doing the same work in different disciplines. Our collaborations and our friendship mean a great deal to me.

Kyle Gann has been the most consistent and outspoken advocate for my music. Kyle's insights have often inspired me to new work, and his faith in my music has strengthened my resolve to continue working.

Gordon Wright has always believed in me. He commissioned and conducted my music when few others were interested. As mentor, wilderness travel companion, next-door neighbor, and sauna mate, Gordon has taught me much about music and about life.

Leif Thompson has been a trusted musical confidant—the person with whom I've shared my work in its earliest stages, and who has helped me clarify many of my most important musical questions.

Over the years I've been blessed to work with many wonderful performing musicians whose gifts have revealed things in my music that I couldn't have imagined were there.

From early on Amy Knoles, Robin Lorentz, and Robert Black have been with me, nurturing my music as it first began to coalesce. They still understand it better than I do.

Allen Otte has been my partner in wide-ranging musical inquiries. I can always rely on Al for unexpected insights, and to challenge me with essential musical truths.

JoAnn Falletta has been an important proponent of my music, performing and recording my orchestral works with precision, care, and genuine conviction.

As a composer, Paul Dresher is an admired and respected colleague. As a performer, he's been extraordinarily generous in commissioning and touring my music with his dynamic ensemble.

Working with Steven Schick always reminds me that music must have real meaning in life. Beyond Steve's musical and intellectual brilliance, a shared love of good pitching and single-malt whisky sweetens our friendship.

In Alaska my closest musical friend is Scott Deal. Scott's irrepressible sense of adventure makes it a joy to experiment freely, and his unique musicianship makes it possible for me to work at the highest level here at home.

Jim Culley, Rusty Burge, Stuart Gerber, Michael Fowler, John Kennedy, and Charles Amirkhanian each in his own way has been a special champion of my work.

Paul Tai and Paul Marotta at New World Records, Jim Fox at Cold Blue Records, and Foster Reed and Tom Welsh at New Albion Records have all helped bring the music to a wider audience.

I also want to thank James Tenney, Pauline Oliveros, and Peter Garland for encouraging me to publish these writings, and Sabine Feisst and Mitchell Morris, whose writings have expanded my own thinking about my work.

Frank J. Oteri, editor of *NewMusicBox*, first published a number of these writings and helped shape this book. Composer, writer, and evangelist for new music of all kinds, Frank is a remarkable polymath and a delightful friend.

Mike Dunham of the *Anchorage Daily News* and Gayle Young, editor of *Musicworks*, published several of the pieces and offered valuable suggestions on early drafts of the manuscript.

Paul Zinman of Soundbyte Productions and Nathaniel Reichman have performed aural alchemy for many of my recordings and performances. Todd Tarantino has been meticulous in preparing numerous scores and parts for performance.

Dennis Keeley, whose photographs grace these pages, is a life-long friend who has shared many important moments and places with me.

Randall Davidson is a kindred composer peer, an attentive friend, and a wise advisor on questions of every kind.

Fred and Alexandra Peters are the most generous of friends. Time and again the open door at their lovely home has provided me with a warm and comfortable base camp in the wilds of Manhattan.

I want to express my gratitude to Meet the Composer, the Foundation for Contemporary Performance Arts, the Aaron Copland Fund for Music, the American Music Center, the Rockefeller Foundation, the Paul Allen Foundation, and the Rasmuson Foundation for their generous and timely support of my work.

I'm also deeply grateful to John Schaefer, Ralph Jackson, and Don Gillespie, whose belief in my work has meant so much to me.

Most of all I want to thank my wife and soul mate, Cynthia. She is my best editor and most patient advisor. I can't imagine where I would be without her love and her constant faith in building and sharing a life with me.

Winter Music

The author with Aeolian harp. Photo by Fran Durner, Anchorage Daily News

The Place Where You Go to Listen

*Songs are thoughts which are sung out with the breath when
people let themselves be moved by a great force, and ordinary
speech no longer suffices.*

*When the words that we need shoot up of themselves,
we have a new song.*
—Orpingalik, a Netsilik elder

They say that she heard things.

At Naalagiagvik, The Place Where You Go to Listen, she
would sit alone in stillness. The wind across the tundra and the
little waves lapping on the shore told her secrets. Birds passing
overhead spoke to her in strange tongues.

She listened. And she heard. But she rarely spoke of these
things. She did not question them. This is the way it is for one
who listens.

She spent many days and nights alone, poised with the deep
patience of the hunter, her ears and her body attuned to everything around her. Before the wind and the great sea she took
for herself this discipline: always to listen. She listened for the
sound, like drums, of the earth stirring in ancient sleep. She listened for the sound, like stone rain, as rivers of caribou flooded
the great plain. She listened in autumn for the echo of the call of
the last white swan.

She understood the languages of the birds. In time, she learned
the quiet words of the plants. Closing her eyes, she heard small
voices whispering:

I am uqpik. I am river willow. I am here.
I am asiaq. I am blueberry. I am here.

The wind brought to her the voices of her ancestors, the old ones, who taught that true wisdom lives far from humankind, deep in the great loneliness.

As she traveled she listened to the voices of the land, voices speaking the name of each place, carrying the memories of those who live here now and those who have gone.

As she listened, she came to hear the breath of each place—how the snow falls here, how the ice melts—how, when everything is still, the air breathes. The drums of her ears throbbed with the heartbeat of this place, a particular rhythm that can be heard in no other place.

Often she remembered the teaching of an old shaman who spoke of *silam inua*—the inhabiting spirit, the voice of the universe. *Silam inua* speaks not through ordinary words but through fire and ice, sunshine and calm seas, the howling of wolves, and the innocence of children, who understand nothing.

In her mind she heard the words of the shaman, who said of *silam inua*: "All we know is that it has a gentle voice like a woman, a voice so fine and gentle that even children cannot be afraid".

The heart of winter: She is listening.

Darkness envelops her—heavy, luminous with aurora. The mountains, in silhouette, stand silent. There is no wind.

The frozen air is transparent, smooth and brittle; it rings like a knife blade against bone. The sound of her breath as it freezes is a soft murmuring, like cloth on cloth.

The muffled wing beats of a snowy owl rise and fall, reverberating down long corridors of dream, deep into the earth.

She stands motionless, listening to the resonant stillness. Then, slowly, she draws a new breath. In a voice not her own, yet somehow strangely familiar, she begins to sing.

Resonance of Place

Confessions of an Out-of-Town Composer

(1992–96)

Landscape is the culture that contains all human cultures.
—Barry Lopez

The places we live in resonate within us. The sounds around us—the songs of birds, the cries of animals, the rhythms of the seasons and the reverberations of the elements—all echo in the music of a place.

The rich diversity of music around the world is a result of people living for centuries in harmony with their own physical and cultural geographies. Today, even in urban areas where musicians have little or no intimate experience of the natural world, there are still qualities of music unique to specific places. In large measure these qualities arise from the vitality and persistence of ethnic traditions. But how did the sounds and rhythms of the earth influence the birth and growth of those traditions? How does where we live influence the music we make? And how might closer listening to the music of place contribute to a renewal of human music and cultures?

My place is Alaska. For many years now I've lived and worked in the northern interior. Not surprisingly I've given some thought to these questions and to the question of what it means at the dawn of the millennium to make a life as a composer so far from the capitals of global commerce and culture.

Like many of my generation of middle-class North Americans I grew up in several different places, amid relatively homoge-

This essay evolved from a lecture I presented on numerous occasions from 1992 to 1996. It has previously appeared in print in several forms and was the basis of a program produced for the Alaska Public Radio Network.

neous suburban surroundings. In my twenties I sought and found my spiritual home in Alaska and I made a deep commitment to pursue my life's work here. Through sustained listening to the unique resonances of this place I've aspired to make music that belongs here, somewhat like the plants and the birds—music informed by worldwide traditions but music that can best, perhaps only be made here. As a composer in the far North I've come to feel increasingly removed from cosmopolitan musical fashions. After all, the only human music that has been here for long is the music that grew here—the chants and dance songs of the Yup'ik, Iñupiat, Unangan (Aleut), Athabascan, Tlingit, Haida, and other Native peoples. There's a sense (an illusion, perhaps, but exciting nonetheless) that one might discover a new kind of music here— music that somehow resonates with all this space and silence, cold and stone, wind, fire and ice.

A RESERVOIR OF SILENCE

There are silences so deep
you can hear
the journeys of the soul,
enormous footsteps
downward in a freezing earth.
—John Haines

In his remarkable book *The Tuning of the World*, the Canadian composer R. Murray Schafer uses the term "keynote" to mean the sonic ground of a particular place and time, the sound against which all other sounds are perceived. We rarely listen to these keynotes. Often they're most conspicuous in their absence. On the coast the keynote is the roar of surf. On city streets and highways it's the roar of the automobile. And the keynote of most modern houses and buildings is the 60-cycle electrical hum.

The keynote of the northern interior is silence. The rivers are frozen much of the year. Snow mutes the land. And the wind is calm more often than not. With human and animal life spread sparsely over sprawling distances, sound is the exception. This pervasive stillness can attune the ear in extraordinary ways. As Schafer observes: "In the special darkness of the northern winter . . . the ear is super-sensitized and the air stands poised to beat with the subtle vibrations of a strange tale or ethereal music."

I listen for that music: in the growl of boot steps on fresh snow at 40 below zero, in the haunted cry of a boreal owl, in the luminous dance of the aurora borealis across a moonless sky.

Listening carefully we realize (as John Cage reminded us) that silence doesn't literally exist. Still, silence is a powerful and mysterious sound image. And in a world going deaf amid a technological din, silence is a profound metaphor of the spirit. Much of Alaska is still filled with silence and one of the most persuasive arguments for the preservation of the original landscape here may be its spiritual value as a great reservoir of silence.

To be immersed in this silence is to be near the heart of this place. As each sound passes, the silence returns—a vast and ancient silence that envelops the landscape like a frozen ocean of Time. Straining, you can almost hear the reverberations of the earth stirring in sleep, the movements of mountains, the passing of a cosmic storm—sounds so profound that you hear them not with your ears but in the oldest, darkest core of your being. And other sounds, faint and distant, suspended in air like the remembered sunlight of a summer afternoon ten thousand years past.

THE FIRST MUSICIANS AND
THE MUSICAL LANDSCAPE

. . . birds become ideas . . . Birds are not like ideas—that is a literary simile. They are ideas.

Apart from the bird itself, what of the habitat through which it moves, and to which it returns unseen? If all creatures are possible ideas . . . the habitat is for us the outward form of the whole space of the mind. —Paul Shepard

9

Hermit Thrush phrases in *songbirdsongs*

For me it began with birds. Olivier Messiaen called them "the first musicians". When I was coming of age as a composer the songs of birds stirred memories and longings deep within me. The extended cycle *songbirdsongs* (1974–79) was my attempt to bring something of the magic of the music of birds into my own. I spent many days and hours in the field—listening, sketching, and (as Annie Dillard says) "learning the strange syllables, one by one." But in these miniatures for piccolos and percussion my concern was not so much precise transcription of the pitches and rhythms of bird songs. Instead I tried to find my own free *translations* of those marvelous languages that we humans may never really understand.

Gradually my settings of bird songs began to grow. The songs of the hermit thrush, varied thrush, and Swainson's thrush found their way into *A Northern Suite* (1979–81), a set of five tone-paintings for chamber orchestra. In this music I set fragments of bird songs amid broad, slowly changing textures of sustained tones that I hoped would echo something of the expansive Alaskan landscapes.

In time landscape became the primary metaphor for my music. Wilderness landscapes were my touchstones for works such as *Night Peace* (1977) and *The Far Country of Sleep* (1988). The latter was composed in memory of Morton Feldman, a composer whose music has had a profound influence on my own. Although he was an unrepentant urbanite, Feldman's music is for me haunted by the ideal of the sublime landscape. The title of my homage to him is borrowed from a poem by John Haines that evokes in my mind not only the unbroken spaces and silences of the Arctic, but the ultimate wilderness, Death, through which we all must pass.

Dream in White on White (1992) (for harp, string quartet, and string orchestra) began as a tundra landscape, painted in the "white" tones and non-tempered intervals of Pythagorean diatonic tuning. The monochromatic sonorities (abundant harmonics, open strings, mutes, and no vibrato) and the broad textures

From A Northern Suite

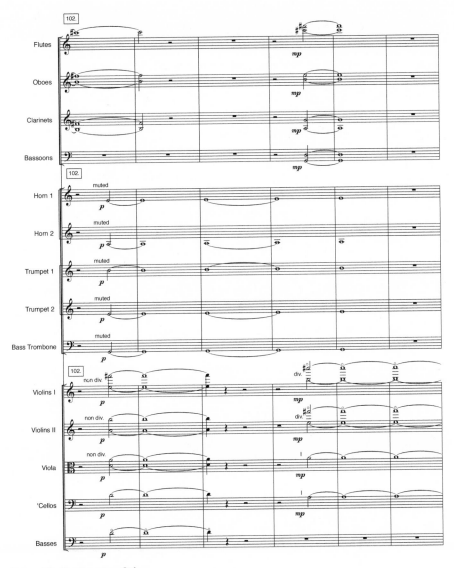

From The Far Country of Sleep

13

From *Dream in White on White*

14

of this music suggest vast white country. But in *White on White* I wanted to move away from music *about* place, toward music that *is* place. I wanted not only to portray a natural landscape in music, but to create a musical landscape with an essential coherence in some way equivalent to the wholeness of a real place; music that conveys its own inherently musical sense of place.

WORDS OF THE EARTH

This earth written over with words,
with names, and the names
come out of the ground,
the words like spoken seeds.
—John Haines

In collaboration with the poet John Haines, I composed the choral and orchestral cantata *Forest Without Leaves* (1982–84). The primary source for this music was the text itself. I approached the words of John Haines as I had previously approached my work with the songs of birds: listening carefully for the inherent music of another's language, then translating what I heard in that language into my own.

Haines's words are deeply rooted in the earth. But *Forest Without Leaves* encompasses far more than simple nature images. These poems survey the interrelationships between the natural world and human societies, from pre-history to post-apocalypse. As Haines puts it: In "a world spiritually blighted and physically threatened with destruction", art "becomes, of necessity, revolutionary as it relates to the social organism within which the art must function and from which it obtains much of its material and impulse. . . . Art at its fullest becomes representative of a harmony at rest somewhere between nature and society."

Working on *Forest Without Leaves* I came to understand that in order to become more complete my music must somehow en-

From Forest Without Leaves

compass not only an idyllic vision of the natural world, but the complexity and chaos of contemporary life as well.

WORLD MUSIC AND INTERNATIONALISM

Properly speaking, global thinking is not possible.
—*Wendell Berry*

In the past fifty years, with the advent of widespread sound recordings, our awareness of the world's music has expanded dramatically. Western composers of "art" music have begun to integrate sounds, forms, and instruments from all over the world into their music to an unprecedented extent. We in the post–World War II generation are the first people to have grown up with an awareness of most of the world's music, both living and historical. In this new context, as the composer Peter Garland observes, " 'World music' ceases to be exotic or peripheral: it becomes the heart of a search for a re-casting of values."

While the extent of music available to us is unprecedented, we certainly aren't the first to borrow from other cultures. That practice is as old as humanity. Earlier generations of American composers—among them Henry Cowell, Harry Partch, John Cage, and Lou Harrison—have been pioneers in bringing the music of the whole world into Western music.

The influence of non-Western music has been remarkably healthy in many ways. Western music has been infused with a new vitality and some lovely new musical hybrids have been born. But ironically, our recent passion for the musical traditions of other cultures has coincided with and perhaps unwittingly contributed to the decline of many of those same traditions.

Mass communications and marketing can transform authentic voices into trivialized fashions and commodities. Globalism contains within it the seeds of cultural colonialism. With the noblest of intentions the superficial qualities of ancient traditions are casually appropriated and popularized. Uprooted from place, history, and experience, unique local idioms are quickly homogenized and devoured as fodder for the so-called music industry. Whether the product is cars or computers, hamburgers or compact discs, the voracious arrogance of global commerce is the same. Like our precious remnants of physical wilderness, the cultures of the "developing world" are viewed as storehouses of raw materials and products for exploitation and consumption.

Diversity is an essential characteristic of healthy biological systems. This is an incontrovertible law of nature. The same is true of human cultures. Artistic pluralism is necessary not just to cultural vitality. It is also quite literally a matter of cultural survival. Any new "global" vision of culture must be based on an unshakable commitment to cherish and sustain the diversity of local cultures. The degree to which we do this will reflect our fundamental attitudes toward one another and toward the earth itself. Ultimately our own survival as a species may depend on our respect for and defense of cultural and biological diversity.

Like the first photographs of the Earth taken from space, recordings of music from other cultures have given us in the West a radically new perspective on the world of music. But as Wendell Berry observes: "Look at those photographs of half the earth, taken from outer space, and see if you recognize your neighborhood. If you want to see where you are, you will have to get out of your space vehicle, out of your car, off your horse, and walk over the ground."

The same may be said for truly *hearing* where we are.

THE INDIGENOUS CONTEXT

The longer I walk the ground of my home, Alaska, the more I admire and respect the music of its indigenous peoples, music that resonates with the experience of living and listening in this place for thousands of years. The rest of us have much to learn from the First Peoples of the North. And the survival of Native cultures in the face of the incredible social upheavals confronting them is a continuing source of hope and inspiration.

In 1986 I was invited to compose a score for the public television series "Make Prayers to the Raven." Adapted from Richard Nelson's book of the same title, the films in this series offer an intimate view of the lifeways and spiritual beliefs of the Koyukon Athabascan people of Interior Alaska. Most of the music I composed for the films came from my own experience listening to the natural sounds of the Interior, which is also my home. But for two brief sequences I adapted and arranged two songs composed and sung by Joe Beetus, a Koyukon elder. At first I was reluctant to work with these songs, out of respect for their completeness and integrity. But Joe agreed to "loan" them to me, and in the context of the films this seemed appropriate. Learning and working with these melodies, I was delighted and fascinated by their free-floating tonalities and their subtle, shifting meters and rhythms.

A few years later I was asked to compose music for a film about the geese that nest on the deltas of the Yukon and Kuskokwim Rivers and their importance to the lives of the Yup'ik Eskimo people of that region. Again I incorporated indigenous music into my score, "borrowing" songs from the Yup'ik dancer, singer, and drummer Chuna McIntyre and others. This music eventually became the *Five Yup'ik Dances* for solo harp.

More recently my friend Ari Vahan asked me to compose two songs on poems she had written in her native Gwich'in dialect. Ari used these songs at a summer camp to teach young Athabascan children a little of the language of their ancestors. Together with a short Dena'ina (Kenai Peninsula Athabascan) song remembered by the late Peter Kalifornsky, and with my settings of Joe Beetus's songs from *Make Prayers to the Raven*, these became the *Five Athabascan Dances* for harp and percussion.

Traditionally the Yup'ik and Athabascan melodies on which these pieces are based would be sung in unison, with no harmony or counterpoint. As a Western composer I've added varia-

From *Five Athabascan Dances*

tions, countermelodies, ostinati, introductions, interludes, and codas—transforming them into a different kind of music, somewhat far removed from their original sounds and cultural contexts. In doing so, I trust I've done no harm. I've been drawn to work with these songs out of my long admiration for Native music and culture, and I hope my treatment of them conveys my profound respect for their origins.

Native American stories were the primary sources for *Giving Birth to Thunder, Sleeping with His Daughter: Coyote Builds North America* (1986–90), my first theatrical collaboration with the writer Barry Lopez. The protagonist of these stories is Old Man Coyote, the Trickster-Creator-Seducer-Fool of oral traditions from the Southwest to the Great Plains to the Northwest Coast.

I began my musical life as a rock 'n' roll drummer. And I've long admired Native drumming traditions from the Nez Perce to the Iñupiaq, as well as the percussion music of Cage, Harrison, Cowell, and other American composers. Not surprisingly, then, the music for *Coyote Builds North America* began with percussion. I wanted to combine the energy of rock with the rhythmic complexity of "art" music. But although some of the percussion instruments (tom-toms, rattles, log drum, and the like) occur in Native American music, I chose not to borrow directly from those traditions.

The Coyote stories are rich with the wisdom and humor of the Native peoples of North America. At the same time Coyote is an archetypal figure who appears in different incarnations throughout the world. In China, he's Monkey. In Africa, he's Spider. Elsewhere he's Fox, Harlequin, or Hare. In my home country of Interior Alaska, he's Raven.

Like all great expressions of the human spirit, Coyote transcends culture. These stories are as universal as a novel by Tolstoy or a symphony by Beethoven. Ultimately—like the earth, the water and the air—Coyote belongs to no one and to everyone.

In the words of a Pawnee song:

From *Coyote Builds North America*

We are here on this earth,
a tribe—
anybody.

BEYOND LANDSCAPE

Deep within the human imagination we sense that nature itself is our deepest source of creative forms and energy. And most of us tend to think of landscape as the ultimate ground of nature. To be sure, the ideal of the sublime landscape has inspired many great works of music, art, and literature. Yet there's another sense in which the notion of landscape limits our understanding and experience of place.

Reflecting on the evolution of his own thought, the human ecologist Paul Shepard writes of his realization that "the world-as-picture was on one hand geared to the superficiality of taste and on the other an outcome of a Renaissance mathematical perspective that tended to separate rather than join the human and the nonhuman. The landscape was an inadequate nexus."

Shepard's dissatisfaction with landscape is more than splitting semantic hairs. It speaks to the very core of our relationship with the world in which we live. When Barry Lopez speaks of landscape as the culture that contains all human cultures, the word is full of rich connotations derived from a lifetime of intimate personal experience in the landscape. But for many of us landscape is something we view from a distance: within the frame of a painting or a photograph, on a television set or a movie screen, or through the window of a speeding automobile. Such encounters with place can be thought provoking and inspiring. All too often they're sadly superficial.

In whatever sense we understand the concept of landscape, landscape alone is no substitute for the authentic personal experience of fully *being* in a place. As with any true intimacy, this takes time. We can view a landscape in a matter of seconds. But it can take a lifetime to truly know a place.

TOWARD SONIC GEOGRAPHY

They define space more by sound than sight.
Where we might say, "Let's see what we can hear",
they would say, "Let's hear what we can see."
—Edmund Carpenter

Over the years my music has led me beyond landscape painting with tones into the territory of "sonic geography"—a region that lies somewhere between place and culture, between human imagination and the world around us. My first exploration of this territory was *Earth and the Great Weather: A Sonic Geography of the Arctic.* In 1989 I was commissioned to create a half-hour work for public radio. I began by returning to the Arctic National Wildlife Refuge, a country in which I've traveled over the past three decades. The result was a sound-piece that combined the music of an Aeolian harp with Iñupiaq drums and recordings of the natural elements—wind across tundra, ice melting, migratory birds calling, thunder rolling on mountaintops. Floating through this geography were voices, intoning and whispering litanies of names—the names of places, plants, birds, and other animals—in English, Latin, and Iñupiaq. I imagined the Iñupiaq place names and their English translations as sonic landmarks for the listener traveling through this country of the mind.

Even before completing the radio piece, I realized I'd begun something much larger than I'd first understood. From that beginning *Earth and the Great Weather* grew, and along with it my understanding of sonic geography. The shorter radio piece became an evening-length performance work. The wind harps were replaced by a quartet of strings, electronically expanded to produce textures of orchestral dimensions. The geography encompassed by the work also expanded, crossing the Arctic Divide into the boreal forest—the physical, cultural, and spiritual homeland of the Gwich'in Athabascan people.

And the scale of the drumming grew. Rising like mountain ranges above the aeolian plains are three pieces for four drummers. These quartets were constructed of rhythmic cells drawn from Iñupiaq and Athabascan dance and ceremony, which I've admired and studied for many years.

The earth speaks to us and we speak to it through names—the names we give to places, plants and animals, to the weather, the seasons, the directions, and the elements. The principal text of Earth and the Great Weather is a series of Arctic Litanies, composed entirely of names. In fact the entire work grew from the images inspired by a single name: Naalagiagvik—"The Place Where You Go to Listen"—the Iñupiaq name for a place on the coast of the Arctic Ocean. The Iñupiat and the Gwich'in Athabascan people have lived in the Arctic for centuries, and the names with which they speak to the world around them constitute an authentic poetry of place.

The title of the work comes from a song by the Iglulik shaman, Uvavnuk.

The great sea
has set me adrift.
It moves me like the weed in a great river.
Earth and the great weather move me,
have carried me away,
and move my inward parts with joy.

Alaska's Native peoples have long known that there are places on this earth that are especially powerful and sacred. I believe the place we now call the Arctic National Wildlife Refuge is among the most sacred of places and that no amount of material wealth can justify violating or desecrating it. Still Earth and the Great

From *Earth and the Great Weather*

Weather is not an intentionally political work. I composed it to celebrate a sacred place, and to invite the listener on an aural journey through its landscapes, both imaginary and real.

MUSIC, TECHNOLOGY, AND THE SOUNDSCAPE

In our hurried, visually oriented society few of us take time to listen beneath the surface noise of life. Listening attentively to the music of the natural world, we encounter a different sense of time than in most human music. The rhythms are more subtle and complex. The tempos can be extreme—very much faster and very much slower than most of our music. And ultimately the music of nature leads us away from notions of tempo and rhythm (which imply the temporal "grid" of a regular beat), to a more direct experience of the larger flow of time.

Attentive listening to natural sounds can also expand our understanding of musical meaning. Human music is generally a semantic phenomenon in which the relationships *between* sounds mean as much as the sounds themselves. But sounds as they occur in nature are not symbols, subjects, or objects. They represent nothing other than themselves. They simply *sound*. The greatest power and mystery of natural sounds lie in their immediate and non-referential nature. If we listen carefully enough we may occasionally hear them just as they are.

The voices of wind and water, the primal music of bird songs and animal cries, remind us of the power of this deeper, simpler mode of listening. Listening to the resonances of the soundscape, we rediscover those mysterious connections between the sounds we make and the larger, older world to which we belong. In time our music may come to be defined not by the symbolic strictures of musical semantics or by the limits of our inventiveness, but only by the limits of our experience listening to the world around us.

Electronic technology now makes it possible to manipulate

and compose with any sound the way one would compose for musical instruments or human voices. But just as the mass media can turn vital indigenous voices into commercial commodities, microphones and recording devices allow us to transform living sounds into raw material for our manipulations. Removing a sound from its original setting and placing it in a "musical" setting can celebrate the sound, or it can trivialize both the sound and the music.

Like all human endeavors, music derives its fundamental forms and energy from our response to the world around us. And the parallels between the sounds of other-than-human nature and our own music suggest rich possibilities. Our music can be enriched not only by natural sounds themselves, but also by the forms and processes of nature. As John Cage observed, we have much to learn by imitating "nature in her manner of operation." Along with other artists in the past century Cage has opened our ears to the entire world of sound as music. His radical definition of music as "sounds heard" parallels the scientific insights of ecology, quantum physics, and chaos theory, which have given us a renewed awareness and deeper understanding of the intricate interrelationships of everything around us.

NEW INDIGENOUS MUSICS

I will build a new culture, fresh as a young animal.
It will take time . . . It will take time . . . There will be time.
—R. Murray Schafer

Composers and sound artists all over the world are turning their ears to the music of the earth. These artists have steeped themselves in the natural and cultural landscapes of the places they call home, embracing them as fundamental elements of their life's work. In doing so they are practicing a new kind of artistic regionalism. This new regionalism is anything but provincial in character. Conversant with the broadest range of music from other times and places, these artists consciously choose to listen and work with the sources most closely at hand. In doing so they are helping to create genuine alternatives to a global monoculture.

A constant reality for those of us who choose to live and work in the hinterlands is isolation. We have few peers close at hand with whom we can talk shop and compare notes. Skilled musicians eager to perform new music are scarce and there are fewer opportunities for performances than in the major urban centers. Still, because the history and institutions of the dominant culture are somewhat less deeply entrenched, it may be that composers, writers, and other artists who live and work closer to the land have a special contribution to make toward revitalizing Western culture.

This is not self-conscious primitivism or simplistic isolationism. It is a vital current in the flow of human culture and consciousness. The explorations and discoveries of the recent past have given us a wealth of new artistic and technical tools to work with. But to fulfill that most basic creative need—to rediscover and re-create order between ourselves and the world around us—we must also continually renew our connections with older, deeper sources.

There may be a certain naïveté in this attitude. But a little naïveté can be a very healthy thing. Much of the work we produce from these beginnings will be tentative, especially when compared with the facile gloss and technical brilliance of more cosmopolitan styles and genres. But in time more complete and mature statements will follow.

Writing about a festival of indigenous Hispanic music in New Mexico, Peter Garland expresses his amazement at "the integrity and survival of this music . . . its authenticity in the overall fabric of culture and life-ways; and its authentic geographical place— qualities which are sadly disappearing from regional musics in the face of national and international media." Garland goes on

to observe, "This kind of regionalism is now no longer an isolated one, but one that embraces its own values—in the face of
everything else in the world."

As we confront the mass media, commercial culture, and
"everything else in the world," music like this reminds us that we
can and we must rediscover and reclaim our own musical iden-
tities. As we come to understand better *where* we are, we come
to understand more fully *who* we are. Respecting and cherishing
music from all other times and places, we can begin to make new
indigenous music—here and now.

Sonata for Bassoon and Piano

After finishing my undergraduate studies at Cal Arts in 1973, I faced the obvious but intimidating question: "What next?"

I applied and was accepted for graduate school at three institutions, but none of them quite seemed to fit. My interview with the chairman of composition at one of the schools was especially memorable.

"The committee and I have reviewed your scores and listened to your tapes," he said. "Your work is interesting, but we're concerned about your apparent lack of a sound traditional background."

He continued: "If you pursue graduate studies here, you will work with me. The first thing I will have you do is write a composition in a traditional form, for instance a sonata for bassoon and piano."

At that moment, for me, the interview ended.

A few days later I sent the following to the Chairman of Composition.

Sonata for Bassoon and Piano
(for Professor X)

My traditional background
is sound
—an intense love for sound
and very little else.

The power of sound
will always be more important to me
than any techniques, conventions or traditions.

Make a joyful noise
and
let the sound resound!

It never occurred to me that I might go to graduate school to prepare for a future position in academia, or to make professional connections to advance a career. Composing and life experience seemed more important to me. So I abandoned the idea of pursuing further institutional studies and eventually found my way to Alaska, where I traveled in the wilderness, worked as a guide and an environmental activist, and studied bird songs and indigenous music. These experiences served as my graduate school.

In Alaska I began composing with a sense of freedom I doubt I would have felt in New York or Europe or even in California. But my opportunities to hear what I composed were limited. Fortunately Gordon Wright took an interest in me. As Gordon is fond of saying: "I haven't always understood your music, but I've always believed in you." No young composer could have asked for more.

During his tenure as music director of the Fairbanks Symphony Orchestra and the Arctic Chamber Orchestra, Gordon conducted numerous performances of my music. He and the musicians of the orchestras were extraordinarily generous and patient in allowing an upstart young composer to learn at their expense. For the better part of a decade, I was the timpanist and principal percussionist with these two ensembles. This was an opportunity that would not have been available to me in most places. The experience of being inside rehearsals and performances of Bach, Haydn, Mozart, Beethoven, Brahms, Schumann, Franck, Dvořák, Debussy, Bartók, and Stravinsky taught me many practical lessons in composition and orchestration. Touring with the Arctic Chamber Orchestra took me to communities all over the North and exposed me directly to Alaska Native music, dance, stories and visual art. With the symphony I established an annual series of new music concerts, which allowed me (as both percussionist and conductor) to learn and perform many new works.

At the same time I worked in public radio. For several years I produced a weekly program devoted to new music that sometimes included interviews with composers. My conversations with Morton Feldman, Dane Rudhyar, and Conlon Nancarrow were especially memorable experiences. I also recorded interviews with Peter Garland, Paul Dresher, Ingram Marshall, Glenn Branca, Jim Fox, Daniel Lentz, and other composers of or closer to my own age. After several years in near total isolation, this gave me a welcome sense of connection with a widespread community of creative musicians. In time I began working with my own ensemble, bringing outstanding new musicians to Alaska to rehearse, perform, and record *Coyote Builds North America* and, later, *Earth and the Great Weather*.

Throughout these journeyman years, my friendship with Lou Harrison was a lifeline. Although I never studied with him formally, I learned more from my time with Lou than from any of my institutional studies. Intonation, form, notation, orchestration, history—Lou was bursting with knowledge, and he was always teaching. Most importantly, he was an inspiring model of how to live, without regret or bitterness, as an uncompromising independent composer.

songbirdsongs (1974–79)

These small songs are echoes of rare moments and places where the voices of birds have been clear and I have been quiet enough to hear. Now and then this magic finds me (like one of Harry Partch's Lost Musicians) wandering in search of my own voice.

If I have abdicated the position of Composer (with a capital "C") it is because, like E. E. Cummings, "I'd rather learn from one bird how to sing than teach ten-thousand stars how not to dance." After all, what do we really create but answers to Creation?

This music is not literal transcription. It is translation. Not imitation, but evocation. My concern is not with precise details of pitch and meter, for too much precision can deafen us to such things as birds and music. I listen for other, less tangible nuances. These melodies and rhythms, then, are not so much constructed artifacts as they are spontaneous affirmations.

No one has yet explained why the free songs of birds are so simply beautiful. And what do they say? What are their meanings? We may never know. But beyond the realm of ideas and emotions, language and sense, we just may hear something of their essence. From there, as Annie Dillard suggests, we can begin "learning the strange syllables, one by one."

A Composition Lesson

Music is where you find it.

For ten years Gordon Wright was my neighbor in the spruce forest on the outskirts of Fairbanks. Early one Sunday Gordon dropped by my cabin. I'm not a morning person and Gordon was surprised to find me already sitting at my desk, looking very intent.

"What are you working on?" he asked.

"Oh, it's a piece for flute choir," I sighed. "It kept me up most of the night."

"What seems to be the problem?"

Over a hot cup of coffee I showed Gordon the sequence of chords I had sketched out. "I like the sound of these," I complained. "I just can't figure out what to do with them."

Gordon took a sip and gazed slowly around the room. Finally his eyes settled on my refrigerator, which was covered with bright blue paisley wallpaper. After a long, pensive silence he said:

"Your chords are nice. But flutes like lots of notes and squiggles and curlyques . . .

"Just write your refrigerator!"

That's exactly what I did.

John Haines and the author. Photo by Charles Backus

Forest Without Leaves (1984)

Just as music can be language, language can be music. Without a sense of music, the words of the poet ring hollow. And without the resonance and meaning of language, music loses some of its deepest qualities. The composer and the poet are relative upstarts. From the beginning of human history they sang with one voice. It's only recently that we have come to regard them as separate. Reunited, they can embody strange and powerful new voices, voices that speak urgently to our time.

In his book *The Magic of Tone and the Art of Music*, the late Dane Rudhyar observes: "Man can sound in a physically-concrete manner (through words charged with dynamic, image-evoking energy) the fundamental tone of culture in the making. He can act as the sacromagical poet or bard. He can use Sound as carrier wave to communicate the regenerative answer to the new human need."

That answer is quite literally on the tips of our tongues. But for it to be clear, every word must be fully intelligible, in all its shades of imagery and meaning.

Any composer who sets out to add tones to a text of integrity faces a formidable challenge. As language, the words are complete in and of themselves. Yet when they are spoken, their inherent music seems to cry out for the added resonance of singing voices and instruments. The composer's challenge, then, is to enhance that inherent music without impairing the imagery or meanings of the words. This demands a serious obligation of fidelity to words not only as sound, but also as language. The common conventions of "setting words to music"—forcing them into rigid meters, formulaic harmonies, architectural forms, and

This essay is a distillation of a longer lecture given in Sitka, Anchorage, and Fairbanks in conjunction with the first performances of *Forest Without Leaves*, a cantata composed in collaboration with the poet John Haines. It first appeared in print in *Ear* magazine.

37

essentially instrumental melodies—are simply inappropriate. Instead, the composer must search for the music *within* the words.

Of course this is not a new idea. It is as old as human speech and music. Monteverdi spoke of his vocal music as "the servant of speech". Several centuries later Harry Partch rearticulated this as his ideal of "corporeality": "to disclose a manner of impressing the intangible beauty of tone into the vital power of the spoken word, without impairing either." Partch staked his entire life and work on the revival of corporeality and monophony (literally, "one voice"). In the West our rich heritage of monophony includes liturgical chant (in its syllabic, non-melismatic forms), the chansons of the troubadours, Monteverdi's operas, portions of Bach's cantatas, Schubert's lieder, Debussy's *Pelléas et Mélisande*, Schoenberg's *Pierrot Lunaire*, Mussorgsky's songs, Satie's *Socrate*, and virtually all of Partch's music. But despite this richness of monophony, much of Western vocal and choral music of the past four hundred years treats words as mere decoration, ornaments for the composer's preconceived musical ideas. Apparently many composers (including a number of the most revered) have thought nothing of imposing ill-fitting, nonverbal syntax on the spoken word, and purely instrumental conventions on the human voice.

Our music abounds with such aberrations. Think of the single syllable extended for so long that by the time the word is completed its meaning and context have been lost. Think of the ubiquitous misplaced accents, the complex and subtle rhythms of speech forced into ill-fitting meters and square rhythmic patterns, the melodic lines that follow their own geometrical curves rather than the more free-flowing inflections of speech. Used with imagination, such devices can be effective. But their habitual and indiscriminate use betrays a lack of sensitivity on the part of the composer to the integrity of language, which leads to the obfuscation of the words.

Think of your own experience listening to operas, oratorios, and art songs of any period. Even when you are fluent in the language, how often can you make out more than a word or two now and again, floating aimlessly amid long soaring lines of vowel-colored mush? It's true that much of this is the result of liberties taken in performance by overly zealous singers. But composers willingly perpetrate such betrayals of their texts.

It's not my intention to rail against flights of imagination or to suggest that music must somehow be bound inextricably to speech. The long line clearly has its place, especially in symphonic or chamber music. And the voice can be used very effectively in essentially instrumental ways. But if there is a text that is more than doggerel, if there are words worthy of our attention, then those words—the natural flow of their rhythms and the curves of their melodies—should be the seeds from which everything grows. Their integrity as language should always be respected. Their sound and sense should always be preserved.

Love the Questions (1997)

John Cage said that in the course of his life and work he gradually came to understand composition "not as the making of choices, but as the asking of questions."

Morton Feldman put it even more succinctly, when he advised simply: "Love the questions."

The most important questions in music and in life may turn out to have many answers, or no answers at all. In any case, the questions may well be more important than the answers.

Varèse had a maxim for composing: "Keep it level, especially in times of invention."

Lou Harrison has written: "When I find myself inspired I enjoy it—but, I try to lay the pencil down, for, if I continue, I know that I shall have to use the eraser in the morning."

Although the music of Cage, Feldman, Varèse, and Harrison sounds nothing alike, all four composers speak of a healthy mistrust of "inspiration," "self-expression," and the artist's ego. In very different ways each of them placed his faith in something larger than his own will and intentions: a deep belief in the power of the music and the sounds themselves.

In my own work I try to follow a similar path. I try to ask as clearly and directly as possible a few essential questions about the music at hand. Once I articulate these questions, my discipline is simply to keep faith with the musical materials, to listen carefully to the sounds and follow wherever they might lead me.

Land of Constant Light
Arctic National Wildlife Range (June 1977)

JUNE 11

It is well past midnight. I stand at the edge of the Arctic Ocean looking north across a thousand miles of ice toward the Pole, and south across fifty windswept miles to the crest of the Brooks Range. Pastel slopes rise to shimmering, ghostlike peaks. A cold, damp wind blows off the pack ice. The low Arctic sun bathes everything in warm, saturated light.

East to west, parallel to the coastline, run miles upon miles of color, stone and shadow. Ranges emerge in the distance, then dissolve in my eyes. A geography of illusion. Arctic mirages.

We're waiting on this small island on the edge of the Beaufort Sea for our bush pilot, Walt Audi, to find time in his hectic summer schedule to fly us out into the Arctic National Wildlife Range. We landed here several hours ago in a twin-engine Otter from Deadhorse, the industrial outpost that's sprung up around the oilfields at Prudhoe Bay, a hundred miles to the west. Meeting our plane were a dozen or so residents of the Iñupiaq village of Kaktovik. They came out not because they were happy to see a new party of backpackers, but because they were glad to see the plane.

In the summer of 1977 I first traveled in the country that was then called the Arctic National Wildlife Range. At the time I was an activist for the Wilderness Society and the Alaska Coalition, working for passage of the Alaska National Interest Lands Conservation Act. When the Act passed in 1980, the Wildlife Range was re-named the Arctic National Wildlife Refuge. The area was expanded and much of it was legally protected as Wilderness. But as of this writing (2004), the refuge is still under threat from oil and gas development on the Arctic Coastal Plain.

My tent-mate on this trip was a lanky, affable fellow from North Carolina named Jack. The leader of our company was Ginny Hill Wood, one of the matriarchs of the environmental movement in Alaska. Her tent mate was Betsy, a sprightly 50-year old from California.

Because of an extended airline strike, Kaktovik has had only two flights a week for quite a while, and the local larders are fast becoming bare. The DEW Line station adjacent to town receives its own military supply flights, but villagers depend on commercial runs to bring in staples to supplement their subsistence hunting, fishing, and gathering. As we climbed out of the plane, crates of food were being unloaded by smiling men, women, and children, and stacked onto a waiting pickup truck. When the cargo compartments were empty, we discovered that half our gear was not on the plane.

So we file into the one-room terminal building ("Barter International Airport") to radiophone Deadhorse in search of the packs. For all we know, they could be back in Fairbanks. But then we're in no hurry. The last we heard Walt was out somewhere near the mouth of the Kongakut River (about sixty miles to the east) picking up a film crew that's been out of for several weeks. So who knows when he'll be able to get to us? It looks like a bivouac at Barter International. The icy wind has driven me back inside. As I stretch out on a dusty plastic seat cushion on the cold, hard floor, I wonder which we'll see first: Walt, or the packs?

JUNE 12

From the air the Arctic Coastal Plain looks like a boundless abstract painting of continental scale. It's a vast wash of delicate hues, from sienna to ochre, etched with the sinuous arms of braided rivers and the angular edges of frost polygons, highlighted by sunlight reflected in countless tundra ponds: an enormous, sweeping gesture of color and endlessly varied texture. We fly up the Okpilak River ("The River with No Willows"), west to the Hulahula (named for its sinuous arms), and over the barren foothills, the bleak Sadelrochit Mountains. Ahead, out of dark clouds, rise twin peaks—Michelson and Chamberlin—at nine thousand feet, the crest of the Brooks Range. We fly on in wind-driven rain, over the icebound Neruokpuk Lakes, following in reverse the route we will travel on foot for the next two weeks. We turn west into the Franklin Mountains, then south up the Canning River to a wide bend in its upper reaches.

Walt banks the little Cessna 206 steeply and touches down on a rough gravel bar. Quickly unloading people and packs, he's off again before the weather closes in completely. Clouds soon swallow the plane, leaving us standing in the dim gray twilight with the only sound the drone of the river. Everything is dreamlike, but we're here at last. Someone remarks that it's 2 a.m. Suddenly I realize how exhausted I am after three full days of "hurry up and wait." Jack and I pitch our tent and fall into our sleeping bags.

We sleep until noon, when the sun drives us from the tent. Our friends are already out climbing. We can just make out their small figures on a ridge high above. Packing a light lunch, we strike out for a nearby peak. Jack is long, lanky, and apparently part mountain sheep. He soon leaves me behind. As he bounds up the slopes and scrambles across rockslides, I trundle on, stopping now and then to take in the sweep of the country. The soft, spongy tundra on these slopes is an ankle-deep mat of caribou lichen, mountain avens, dwarf rhododendron, dwarf birch, and a host of other diminutive plants. At lower elevations, the mountainside is brilliant yellow and violet with the beginning of the riotous summer flowering.

In mid afternoon I finally catch up with Jack, sitting on an outcropping at the top. He ribs me a little about my slow pace. Then we fall into silence. The view is overwhelming. Far below, the river is still choked with large fields of *aufeis* (overflow ice). I look out to the naked peaks all around and beyond into space on a scale I've never known before, space that is almost *too* big. It will take time for me to understand the scale of this place—vast, open, and apparently empty.

Photo by Dennis Keeley

44

We rise and alternately bound and slide down the half-mile drop to camp.

JUNE 13

We begin hiking today. We have about fifteen miles to go, three days walking down the east bank of the Canning River to the confluence with a major sidestream. Our route is straight-forward, so we agree on lunch and camping spots in advance, leaving everyone to their own pace and thoughts. I begin walking under the imposing weight of a sixty-pound pack and the un-familiar feel of country different from anything I've known be-fore, even in Alaska. This is a subtle, somber landscape. Little that I've seen, read, or experienced seems to apply out here. I need to shelve the preconceived notions and unearned emotions, and just walk. Walk, listen, and wait. Slowly, rhythmically, almost mechanically, I place one foot in front of the other in front of the other, again and again. Along the river bars, through the wil-low thickets, up the rocky slopes, across the icy streams. Over and over. The sound, the motion, the simple pleasure of just walking. All day I'm haunted by a song. Somewhere, everywhere, a bird is singing—a high, simple strain. The music is familiar yet strange, like a melody I once knew but had long forgotten until here, now, like an echo I hear it again. Hidden, distant, dreaming.

It is evening, or twilight. We're camped in a bare willow thicket by a small stream that rushes out from a steep-walled canyon. It's been a full day. Five miles out here is a lot farther than it is in any place I've ever hiked before. The others are in their tents. But I can't go to sleep yet. I just can't get enough of this country. So I stand in the evening light, taking it all in. Dull gold rims the peaks to the north. A storm is moving in from the south. Low clouds roll down the valley. It's almost dark. As I stoop to crawl into the tent, I look up to see a rainbow, spanning the breadth of the valley, arching from ridge to ridge. Standing beneath it in deep blue-gray space, I reach up. It dissolves into mist.

JUNE 14

We walk today shrouded in rain and clouds that bring the sweep of the country closer, creating a more indefinite but more intimate space. I walk on, through wind and rain. Inside the shell of my rain gear, things seem even closer. The sound of my breathing melds with the roar of the river, footsteps on wet earth and once again, the hidden bird. This place seems to be composed of repetition, simple repetition of sound, motion and form. And music. Music flows through everything out here—sparse elemental music of stone, wind, rain, water, ice. This is not a music that we might play with instruments. This music is larger than we can understand, and we ourselves are the instruments. I remember T.S. Eliot: "You are the music, while the music lasts."

Sometime after noon we all meet beside a long rockslide. This frozen cascade of stone sweeps down a deep canyon to the edge of a sheer cliff that drops off a hundred feet to the river. We hop and crawl across the boulders. On the other side, before we negotiate the cliff, we decide to rope up. Out here a mistake could be costly. We pick our way along a narrow sheep trail. No one says much. At the end of the ledge, we take the ropes off and continue on at our own paces. It goes unsaid, but we seem to feel a little closer to one another, as though the rope still binds us.

JUNE 15

The weather has lifted today and we walk on following game trails, no trails, gravel bars, talus fans, and willow thickets. We see few animals—an occasional sheep on the slopes, moose browsing in the willows, and small birds flitting here and there. In a muddy thicket by the river Ginny notices wolf tracks and a very fresh bear sign—the tracks of a sow and two cubs. This is definitely not the place to surprise a mother bear, so we crash on through the willows with as much noise as we can muster, then make for higher ground.

On a nearby tundra bench we find a full caribou rack. Although we see few animals we know they're here. This is big, lean country. Unless you're flying, you can't count on seeing many animals. If that's what you're after, go to Denali or someplace else where the animals aren't so wild and so scattered and don't mind being seen. Though the country up here is magnificent, there are higher mountains and more spectacular vistas in the Wrangells, the St. Elias, and the Alaska Range. Don't come here for the weather, either. Even in summer, it reaches everywhere. And there's not much of anyplace to hide. Still, this country has a presence like no other place.

At another high bench I stop to rest behind a large rock, out of the incessant wind for a moment. As I sit munching cheese and crumbled crackers I look across the Canning to the country beyond—country every bit as beautiful, as remote, and as vital to the animals as this country we're walking through now. But the land across the river is unprotected. Somewhere out there (a hundred miles or so to the west) is the Trans-Alaska Pipeline and its eight-hundred-mile corridor that now cuts the Arctic in half. How much of this country will we have the vision and the courage to preserve? How much of it will be given over to pipelines and roads and mines? What will happen to the animals? What will happen to the lives of Native people who depend on them? And what will happen to the Arctic coastal plain here in the Wildlife Range? The oil companies hope it will become the next Prudhoe Bay. But it's the calving grounds of the Porcupine caribou herd. And it's the only portion of the Arctic Coastal Plain that isn't yet open for drilling. Surely we can leave this last corner of the Arctic untouched, for the animals and for its intangible value to the human spirit.

In late afternoon we turn east into an unnamed glacial valley. Another mile brings us to a jewel of a lake at the foot of a steep, boldly sculpted ridge. This will be home for a day or two.

JUNE 16

After a cold "night" we wake to warm morning sun. Jack and I head for an icy dip in the deep turquoise water. Almost numb, we drape ourselves over a large boulder to dry in the sun. The day is clear, the air, warm and still. The number of mosquitoes swells by the hour. The summer hordes are just beginning to hatch. I walk the shore of the lake looking for nesting birds and new flowers. Lying on the soft but brittle caribou lichen, looking at the sky, I think of the country behind and the country ahead of us. Except for the highest peaks, the longest rivers and the largest lakes, this country is nameless. Except for the occasional animal path, this country is trackless. From here our route lies to the east—up this unnamed valley over a route we can imagine no visitors have ever traveled. But the value of this place lies not in blazing a new route or climbing an unclimbed peak. It lies in simply being here. Our deepest need is not to possess this land, but to be possessed by it.

Over supper we share the quiet discoveries of the day as we watch three sheep dance across a precipitous ledge high above us. Across the valley the sun dips behind the mountains. The air grows cold and still.

JUNE 17

The afternoon air is warm and heavy with mosquitoes. I sit quietly on a small ledge, high above the roaring creek. My long lens is focused across the stream on a large nest at the top of a sheer bluff. In it are four ragged blobs of down that occasionally shift about: half-grown peregrine falcon chicks. I've sat here for more than an hour waiting for the adult birds to return. My thoughts have wandered all over these mountains and returned, then wandered again—"Outside," as provincial Alaskans say—and returned again here to the bugs, the sun, and this rock. A persistent cloud of whining wings fills the air around my head. Mosquitoes cover my clothes. Sitting here unprotected I would be free lunch for millions of ravenous little bloodsuckers. But breathing through the headnet is stuffy and the long sleeves and gloves are much too warm. It's hard to believe that the temperature dropped into the twenties last night. Today blisters have begun to rise on my hands and neck from the strong ultraviolet rays of the Arctic sun. This rock absorbs it all. Hanging here exposed to the elements year after year, century after century, through the millennia. Not moving. Not speaking. Not thinking. Just sitting. After a while it occurs to me that I may be keeping the adult falcons away from the nest, so I rise quietly and return to camp.

We can get lost out here, losing our small desires and our small fears. There are moments when we can forget all our memories and all our plans, simply getting up in the morning, living through the day and going to sleep when we're tired. The days are filled with these simple things: eating, drinking, walking, sleeping. Every little event, every little thing matters, each in its own time and place. And we sleep deep, restful, dreamless sleep. There's not much thought of "What would happen if . . . ?" We're so far from help that thoughts like these are largely irrelevant. There are no roads, no phones, no radios. We have only ourselves and one another to depend on. So use your head. Watch where you step. Steer clear of willow thickets. And don't sleep with your food, unless you want to be bear bait. The rest will come as it does.

JUNE 18

We strike camp and hike on up the valley. A warm, buggy morning gives way to a cloudy, buggy afternoon. As we watch a pair of moose browsing in a willow thicket, the sky breaks open. We quickly find a spot on the creek bank and pitch a new camp amid pouring rain and relentless bugs.

At last the rain has stopped. All the willows and tent lines are strewn with soggy clothing, and our spirits are more subdued. Climatically speaking this country is a desert. You wouldn't think so based on today's weather. Still, the feeling here is similar to the deserts of the south. The wind, the space, the silence are similar. Whatever lives here, truly lives. A raven circles high above. The Inuit creator spirit, he soars on endless winds over countless miles to nameless places. Above the highest ridges, in the harshest weather, Raven calls in defiance and affirmation: "I am here. I am alive!"

A full belly and a warm, dry sleeping bag are pure delight tonight. Jack is in top form and has me in stitches with his downhome humor. I unzip the tent door and look out through the netting to dense clouds of bugs and fog. The mountains are gone. The valley has been swallowed up. The other tents are not even visible. Only our small shelter remains at the center of a cold, dark world.

JUNE 19

Today we hike on in low fog, over slippery footing and two major stream crossings. The first crossing—through a roaring side stream—is hip deep. We roll up our pants, loosen our pack belts, rope together, and pick our way through the icy torrent, as a slow-moving human bridge. Our second crossing—through the main creek we've been following—is right through a field of melting aufeis. It feels like walking through the middle of a small glacier. This overflow ice has the same steel-blue color, the same rushing meltwater, the same creaks, groans, pops, and splashes of a large glacier, but in miniature. Soaked and chilled, we make camp on the opposite bank in the middle of the spacious upper basin of our creek. The wind rises, making it colder but holding the promise of clear skies by morning.

JUNE 20

We wake to a clear morning and decide to spend the day climbing. Jack and I scramble up three miles and four thousand feet to a sharp, rocky peak with no name. (The map identifies it only as 7360'.) Most of the way I manage to keep up with Jack, even ahead of him. But about six hundred feet below the summit, the going becomes very steep and arduous. For every two steps I take on the loose slate, I slide back down one step. Jack smells success, shifts into overdrive, and scrambles for the top. Several minutes later I clear the ridge and let out a long hoot that rolls down the steep gullies and echoes off a glacier below. The view from up here equals any I've ever seen, and it's made even better by the work it took to get here. Glaciers, rivers, snowfields, and flank upon flank of mountains stretch away in all directions.

The summit itself is a small inclined platform, just large enough for one. There is no room for movement, so I just sit, listening to the distant drone of cascades and the howl of the wind, watching the changing cloud forms. An avalanche rumbles over the edge of a snowfield and plunges into the valley below. I feel immersed in space, as though I'm sitting at both the top and the center of the world. I feel very small, but part of something inestimably large and old and complete. Before long, snow flurries and high winds chase me off the peak.

JUNE 21

We wake to heavy fog and sporadic rain. After waiting all morning for a break that never comes, we decide to hike on up toward the pass in near zero visibility. Staying close together, we climb for several hours into the fog. When the stone walls around us become too steep to be passable, we realize we must be off our course. Descending a steep, rubble-strewn slope amid swirling snow, we make camp in a cold, gusty draw barely two miles above last night's camp.

Oh, well. It's an evening for celebration anyway. Although there will be no midnight sun for us tonight, it is the summer solstice, the longest day of the year. It's also Betsy's birthday. Ginny presents her with a granola-bar cake, complete with emergency fire-starter candle and rip-stop nylon bow. We huddle around the little gas stove singing "Happy Birthday" in the blowing snow. There's also another, more sobering milestone tonight: The first oil should now be flowing in the Trans-Alaska Pipeline. Alaska will never be the same. As a bit of famous graffiti spray-painted on the Pipeline near Fairbanks asks: "Where will it all end?"

The wind and the snow continue. For the first time in ten days, I fall asleep wondering what the morning will bring.

JUNE 22

While we slept three inches of fresh snow have fallen. It's still snowing and blowing as we begin moving again, up the narrowing valley to a small lake in the high pass.

There's no point in lingering at the top, so we begin picking our way down an old caribou trace, descending slowly over snow turned to slush. We make a tricky crossing of raging Carnivore Creek, crawling gingerly from boulder to tipping boulder. Then we march on for eight soggy miles in steadily worsening weather and rising wind. Up above the snowline the footing wasn't too bad. Down here it's a different story. The boulders and cobbles we traverse are dangerously slick. So we keep a close eye on one another, knowing these are prime conditions for hypothermia and accidents. I'm cold, tired, and soaked to the bone. I know I should be miserable, but somehow I'm not. This is a fine walk and a great day. Hiking these long cold miles I begin to feel that at least for a moment I belong in this place. And this place has become a part of the landscape of my soul.

At last, chilled and exhausted, we slog into the old abandoned research site at Neruokpuk Lakes. Across the rotting ice, through the driving slush, we can just make out the opposite shore. The wind howls, rising even higher. The weather shows no signs of breaking. Although this outpost is an eyesore, none of us complains very much about the scattered oil drums, tractor ruts, and falling-down shacks. We're too tired to really care tonight. Besides, it offers shelter of a sort.

As I sit alone in a dilapidated quonset hut amid rundown machinery and half-used crates of twenty-year-old canned goods, my mind wanders back over the country we've traveled, and on across the great plain to Kaktovik. On to the other villages and DEW Line stations strung sparsely along the Arctic coast, to Prudhoe Bay, down the Pipeline and the Alaska Highway to the Lower 48.

There's a deep self-destructive streak in our collective character that leads us all too often to destroy the very thing we profess to love. Greenie backpackers like me and my friends and pointy-toed Pipeline boomers alike all want our piece of the action, our taste of the frontier. But the more we grab for it, the faster it disappears. If future generations are to know an Alaska that is more than a glorified theme park, we must learn to subdue ourselves, not the land.

JUNE 23

We doze most of the morning on the small Army bunks that line both sides of this dark dungeon of a barracks. The weather rages on. When we can muster enough light, we read. The few paperbacks we brought with us have already made the rounds. But now we have an extensive new library of spy stories, romances, ancient outdoor catalogs, and technical manuals strewn about the lab. Then, behind an old freezer, we make a profound literary discovery—a hundred or so pages from the middle of *Crime and Punishment*. This seems appropriately dark reading to match the weather and our grim storm shelter. We search high and low but can come up with neither beginning nor end for the novel. Still, Jack retires to a dimly lit corner to plunge directly into the depths of Dostoyevsky. Thoreau fails to hold my interest, so I occupy myself by reading between the lines of the "Guest Register," rummaging around in the miscellaneous junk and attempting to dry out my soggy gear.

The weather isn't getting any better. It could stay this way for days. And though we could conceivably live off the decrepit canned goods here, we don't especially relish that prospect. So we begin to ration our remaining food. To top things off, the ice on the lake has begun to break up. Although the temperature hovers around freezing, the high winds have opened up dangerous-looking leads in the ice. Ginny thinks it's already marginal for a landing and we don't expect to see Walt until the weather lifts. By then the lake could be completely broken up. That would mean a forced march back several miles to a large gravel bar on Carnivore Creek where, presumably, he could land.

Despite these gloomy thoughts the company is in high spirits and the conversation is good. After dinner we sit in the largest hovel telling jokes and playing charades. Suddenly we hear a low hum rising out of the wind. We jump up and fling open the door to see Walt's Super Cub descending from the ceiling of dark cloud. In disbelief we watch as he circles once and then touches down, just beyond a gaping breach in the ice. Our journey is over.

JUNE 24

Back in Kaktovik, the others have gone. They left in a mad rush of hurry-ups and goodbyes. I stayed behind to await another group of friends and another trip, down the Kongakut River. Now I walk alone in a dense, chilling fog, among rambling houses, junked machinery, and the ubiquitous fifty-five-gallon oil drums. Dirty snowdrifts lie piled beside the muddy road. A polar-bear skin hangs tightly stretched on a rack above a small clapboard house. A longhaired boy on a three-wheel motorbike buzzes by, splashing through a puddle and racing on toward the airstrip, disappearing into the gray void. An old woman in a bright red, wolf-ruffed parka waddles by—smiling, sweet and toothless. Rock music blares from an open window. The mountains are gone. Over toward the radar towers I can see the dim forms of children chasing a volleyball in the fog, running, laughing. It is well past midnight.

Winter Music

A Composer's Journal (1998–99)

WINTER SOLSTICE 1998

For much of the year, the world in which I live is a vast, white canvas. In the deep stillness of the Solstice, I'm profoundly moved by the exquisite colors of the sub-Arctic winter light on snow. Reading the art critic John Gage's essay "Color as Subject," I'm struck by a parallel between the view out my window and Mark Rothko's use of white underneath the colors in his paintings. Like Rothko's translucent fields, the colors on the snow suggest to me broad, diatonic washes suffused with gradually changing chromatic harmonies. Slowly, faintly, I begin to hear it: Music stripped to its most essential elements—harmony and color floating in space, suspended in what Morton Feldman called "time undisturbed."

CHRISTMAS 1998

A life in music is a spiritual practice. As in many disciplines, my practice sometimes involves fasting. From time to time there are periods in which I listen to no music at all. I feel this as a physical need. During busy periods of performance and teaching I hear a great deal of music. And just as I might feel the need to fast after a period of feasting on rich foods, after several months of intensive listening my ears tell me they need a time of rest from music. As I begin new work, my hope is that fasting may help me to hear sounds I haven't heard before, and to hear familiar sounds with new ears.

In her life and work, Pauline Oliveros practices an extremely difficult discipline: "Always listen." I admire this very much. And though fasting from music might seem to be a retreat from listening, I experience it as a time for listening to silence. Most of us are inundated with music and other sounds these days. I feel very fortunate to live in a place where silence endures as a pervasive, enveloping presence.

NEW YEAR 1999

"Happy New Ears!"
—John Cage

Beginning to sketch a large new orchestral piece, I'm studying the paintings of Rothko and Pollock. Like Cage in music, Pollock made a radical new beginning in the middle of the twentieth century. Both artists opened territories they could only begin to explore during their lives. The questions posed by their work will continue to occupy others for a long time to come.

By contrast, Rothko and Feldman were endings. They both explored intensely private, self-contained worlds. And what Brian O'Doherty said of the one could apply just as well to the other: "Rothko was the last Romantic. But the last of something is usually the first of something else." Which makes me wonder: Is it somehow possible to live and work in that timeless intersection between endings and beginnings?

JANUARY 20

For me, composing is not about finding the notes. It's about losing them.

Although I'm still involved in writing scores, the most difficult thing isn't knowing what to write down. It's knowing what *not* to write down. I hope to discover music that sounds and feels

The author on the trail to his studio. Photo by Charles Mason

elemental and inevitable. And before beginning to write I want to hear as much of the new piece as I can, as it begins to take shape in my mind's ear. This is a slow, sometimes difficult process. But over the years I've learned to trust it, even to savor it. I spend a lot of time thinking, reading, looking at art, walking, listening, sketching, trying to understand the essence of the music. After six weeks in this mode, I now have several pages of notes and sketches for the new piece. But I've yet to start writing out the score.

JANUARY 22

Over the years, I've moved away from working with audible compositional processes (an inheritance of minimalism) toward an increasing focus on the fundamental materials of music: Sound and Time. My work is less and less a matter of performing operations on notes, imposing compositional processes on sounds, or working within a syntax of musical "ideas." I now concentrate primarily on asking questions about the essential nature of the music—what it wants from me, and what it wants to be.

JANUARY 23

Today, I'm forty-six years old. By this time in his life, Ives had lost his physical health and had virtually stopped composing. But Feldman was leaving the dry-cleaning business and moving into his more expansive "middle" period. Pollock was gone. But Rothko was poised on the verge of his major breakthrough into his signature style. That happened in 1950, when he was forty-seven. Among my gifts today: The new score is under way.

JANUARY 24

After this, the lines disappear completely.
—Brian O'Doherty

What is line in music? This is a question I've pondered for many years.

In Pollock's poured paintings long, fluid lines are multiplied into layered fields of perpetually moving stasis and perpetually frozen motion. Much of *In the White Silence* is composed of continuously rising and falling lines layered and diffused into an all-over texture of frozen counterpoint. In that piece it feels as though at last I may have discovered a sense of line that is my own. Now, in the new piece, I'm trying to take a leap I've contemplated for years: to let go of line and figuration altogether. But what will be left?

. JANUARY 25

In the new piece, individual sounds are diffused in a continuous texture, always changing but always with a minimum of what the art critics call "incident." This won't be easy to sustain. James Tenney, Pauline Oliveros, and La Monte Young have all found it. So has Glenn Branca in his recent music for orchestra. And Morton Feldman achieved it most fully in his late orchestral works, *Coptic Light* and *For Samuel Beckett*. Listening to all-over textures, it's difficult to concentrate for long on a single sound. The music challenges us to move beyond syntactical meaning, even beyond images, into the experience of listening within a larger, indivisible presence.

JANUARY 26

Monet's haystacks and waterlillies, Cézanne's *Mont Ste-Victoire*, Rothko's floating rectangles, Diebenkorn's *Ocean Park* landscapes

. . . In the twentieth century painters discovered (or rediscovered) working in series. By freezing a particular motive the artist is free to concentrate on deeper nuances in other dimensions of the work. As Robert Hughes observes: "One sees how absolutely Cézanne despised repetition, and how working *en série* was his strategy for avoiding it."

It occurs to me that my new piece is part of a series of extended orchestral works including *In the White Silence* and *Clouds of Forgetting, Clouds of Unknowing*. Some of the sounds are similar, even identical to those earlier works. But this is very different music. Even within itself, the new piece embraces a series of sorts. Identical formal structures recur from section to section. The temporal relationships between sounds remain the same. Only the sounds themselves change. Rather than moving on a journey through a musical landscape, the experience is more like sitting in the same place as light and shadows slowly change.

The longer we stay in one place the more we notice change.

JANUARY 27

It's 45 below zero and getting colder. But it doesn't matter how cold it is. We're moving toward the light. A month after the winter solstice the days are still very short, but noticeably longer. (We gain another seven minutes each day.) The low arc of the sun over the mountains is slowing expanding in height and breadth.

I'm working steadily and savoring the stillness.

JANUARY 28

The cold deepens. So does the silence. Down the valley, Fairbanks is wrapped in a dense cloud of ice fog. Across the Tanana flats, the peaks of the central Alaska Range have disappeared. But out here in the hills the day is golden. The sun is rimmed in a spectral halo of ice crystals.

The temperature on my afternoon walk is 40 below. The only sound not made by me is the brief whoosh of wings as a lone raven flies past, in a straight line to the South. On the hillside, I encounter a young moose browsing on brittle alder branches. I stop. Speaking softly to her, I bow from the waist and move on, giving her a wide berth. She has enough to contend with just staying warm and fed. They're predicting 50 below or colder tonight.

Back in the studio at the writing table, I'm startled by a bright, metallic ringing—like a small bell. I look up to see a boreal chickadee at the feeder outside my window. In such deep cold and silence, the smallest sounds speak with singular clarity.

After all these years I'm still deeply obsessed with landscape. But the resonance of my musical landscape now is more interior, a little less obviously connected with the external world.

In art and music, landscape is usually portrayed as an objective presence, a setting within which subjective human emotions are experienced and expressed. But can we find other ways of listening in which the landscape itself—rather than our feelings about it—becomes the subject? Better yet: Can the listener and the landscape become one?

If in the past the more melodic elements of my music have somehow spoken of the subjective presence, the human figure in the landscape, in the new piece there's no one present . . . only slowly changing light and color on a timeless white field. I remember the Gwich'in name for a place in the Brooks Range: "In A Treeless Place, Only Snow."

JANUARY 29

The cold hovers in place. The ice fog thickens over Fairbanks. The sun still rises only a few degrees above the horizon, and today it's veiled in frozen mist. The snow is bathed in a strange slate blue–grey light.

Toward the end of a long day in the studio I realize that one of the eight layers in the new piece may be a little too busy and unnecessarily detailed. As always the hard part is knowing what to leave out.

For years, I've kept near the piano my variation on Thoreau's dictum, a reminder of how I try to work: "Believe. Concentrate. Simplify. Simplify. Simplify."

JANUARY 30

This deep winter weather has completely changed the acoustics of this place. A couple of days before the heavy cold settled in, it snowed. Since then the wind hasn't blown at all. So those two inches of fresh powder still rest undisturbed on the branches of the spruce and birch trees. The ice fog has now enveloped the hills. Snow and cloud mute the earth and sky. There's almost no ambient noise. No wind. Fewer people and animals are stirring. The air is less reverberant than usual. But sounds travel farther. On my afternoon walk, the few sounds I hear are vividly present. A distant dog team sounds nearby. My mukluks growl angrily in the soft snow.

FEBRUARY 1

I've taken a couple of days to step back from the new work. The extended weather forecast predicts no change.

FEBRUARY 2

The high temperature at the house today was minus 50. But the clouds have thinned and the sun was back, so I went out for my afternoon walk. Even wearing snow pants, polar mukluks, double mittens, insulated cap with earflaps, and heavy parka with the hood up and the ruff pulled forward, my toes and fingers got cold.

In this extreme weather the air almost becomes a different element—like the vapors of dry ice, like liquid fire. I love it. It makes
me feel alive. Down with Global Warming! Long live the cold and
the dark!

Back at work on the new piece, I concentrate on the organ, the
string orchestra, and the string quartet. Moving at relative speeds
of 2, 3, and 4, these are the slowest of eight tempo layers. Relentlessly diatonic throughout, they are the sonic ground of the
piece. After two days away from the score, the erasing I thought
I might need to do doesn't seem necessary. What I have here is a
new texture. In *White Silence*, all the instruments of a given tempo
layer changed chords together. In the new piece, one white cloud
slowly dissolves one into another, tone by tone. This makes an
unbroken diatonic field from beginning to end, over seventy-five
minutes. To hear the individual tones changing will require very
close listening. I think of these as the brushstrokes—the little
discontinuities that articulate and emphasize the larger continuity of the whole.

The chromatic clouds (the colors floating on the diatonic
ground) are played by three choirs of muted brass and wind instruments, each moving at its own tempo. All the instruments
within a choir change tones together. But many of the written
notes are too long to be played in one breath. So the players are
free to breathe individually, as they choose. Brushstrokes, again.
Those breaths will impart a certain richness to the texture.

FEBRUARY 3

Writing about Rothko, Brian O'Doherty asks, rhetorically:
"Why all this blurring of edges?"

I'm asking myself the same question about the new piece. It
might well be called *Colors on a Diatonic Ground*, or *Light on Snow*.
Both light and snow have soft edges. But despite my fascination
with sounding images, this isn't tone painting. It's music. The

sounds don't grow out of the form. The form of the music grows out of the sounds.

The sounds of *Strange and Sacred Noise* were so complex (machine-gun snare drums, roaring tam-tams, howling sirens, thundering bass drums and tom-toms) that they lent themselves to the decisive articulation of hard-edged, geometric forms. But this new piece is in equal temperament and the sounds are more declarative. So to evoke the atmosphere of continuity and expectancy that I'm after, these blurred edges and more diffuse textures seem right.

A good day in the studio. The thermometer holds steady at 55 below zero.

FEBRUARY 4

I've broken my fast. This evening I boarded a jet in Fairbanks at 45 below and flew North—across the Yukon River, the Brooks Range, and the Arctic Coastal Plain—to Barrow, where it's a balmy 33 below. (Although with the wind chill it's more like 80 below!)

I'm here for Kivgiq, the Messenger Feast: three nights of traditional Iñupiaq drumming, singing, and dancing. Groups from all the Iñupiaq villages in Alaska and four villages in Arctic Canada have come to Barrow for this midwinter festival of feasting, gift giving, and celebration.

After twenty years of listening to this music, it still sounds wonderfully strange to me. Yet it's also strangely familiar. By now I know a few songs, at least roughly. And the angular melodic contours, asymmetrical rhythms, powerful unison choruses, and deep, explosive drums have become integral parts of the soundscape of my life.

Once, passing through a crowded urban airport somewhere down south, amid the noise of rushing travelers, I thought I heard an Iñupiaq drumbeat. Instantly, I was transported home. The memory of the sound of those drums took me there.

These sounds can take us on all kinds of journeys. The high-impact, full-spectrum sound of the drums—reiterated all night long—has an inescapable effect on consciousness. In some ways the effect is similar to rock music. But the rhythms in Iñupiaq music are always at least a little surprising. And even when the phrases are relatively predictable, the basic rhythmic cells—2 + 3 or 2 + 2 + 3—are asymmetrical. To my ears this Iñupiaq "heart-beat" (as it's sometimes called) is both more sophisticated and more energizing than the steady 4/4 backbeat of rock 'n' roll. After a strong dance group from the Arctic coast, even the best rock bands sound rhythmically square.

The dancing tonight goes until 1 a.m.

FEBRUARY 5

Just before noon, out across the tundra, a dirty yellow disc barely nudges itself above the horizon. Its outline is vague. It gives off no warmth.

Fairbanks is at latitude 65 degrees North. Barrow sits at the 71st parallel. The days up here are still considerably shorter than in Fairbanks. But within seven weeks—on the spring equinox—they'll be the same length. In Fairbanks for the past few weeks we've been gaining seven minutes of light every day. Up here the rate of change is twice as fast. Although it's still dark most of the time, Barrow is rapidly spinning toward the light.

Sunrise turns out to have been the brightest moment of the day. In mid-afternoon, I walk the mile or so from the lodge to the new Iñupiat Cultural Center. A vague fog has drifted in from the Arctic Ocean, bathing everything in a soft, blue light. The flatness of the light mirrors the flatness of terrain. The sky feels enormous, all-encompassing. In this blue haze, it's difficult to distinguish the distant horizon. Sky melds with Earth, into an enveloping sphere—the center of which is everywhere, the circumference of which is nowhere. (Isn't that the way a Christian philosopher-saint described God?) Standing, walking, being in such a place, it's not difficult to feel the presence of the spirit world.

On my return walk, my mukluk breaks the crusted snow, sending shards sliding across the surface. They sing like broken glass.

Again, the dancing goes until 1 a.m. During the final performance of the evening, a woman from the audience walks up to join the dancers from Kotzebue. She doesn't notice that a small plastic bag has caught her mukluk and she drags the bag with her into the dance area. The audience finds this quite amusing, especially when she finally notices the bag, shakes it free, and continues dancing.

At that moment one of the young drummers puts down his drum, moves quickly out onto the dance floor, picks up the bag, and stuffs it into his pocket. He returns to the drum line, picks up his instrument, and continues drumming.

All this happens amid smiles and good spirits. But it leaves no doubt about the fact that this is ritual space.

FEBRUARY 6

The day dawns (at 11-something a.m.) clear and colder. My friend Doreen Simmonds (one of my Iñupiaq collaborators on *Earth and the Great Weather*) takes me out to the end of the road, to Point Barrow—the northernmost point in Alaska. The Iñupiaq name for this place is *nuvuk*: "a point of land which juts into the ocean." Although the wind is fairly light and the thermometer probably doesn't read much below minus 30, the cold feels intense. We scan for polar bears, but it would be difficult to see them even if they are there. The low sun floods the ice and snow with a rich pink light. The feeling of endless space is exhilarating. This is what I want to find in music!

Kivgiq is not held every year. It occurs after a prosperous hunting season, when there is enough material wealth to allow for widespread gift giving. At the heart of Kivgiq is Kalukak—the Box Drum Dance. This elaborate ceremony is grounded in the myth of the Eagle Mother, who gave the gift of music and dancing to the People.

This is the final night of the festival, and the Box Drum Dance is the high point of the evening. Traditionally each community on the Arctic coast performs a different variation of the dance. At the last Kivgiq, three years ago, the Kalukak was performed by the dancers from the village of Wainwright. Tonight it's performed by the Barrow dancers.

Before the dancers enter, two men bring out a tall extension ladder. One of them climbs the ladder and lowers a rope that's already been hung in place. A third man brings out the box drum and ties it to the rope where it hangs, swinging freely. The drum is made of plywood, about 1 × 1 × 3 feet in dimension. It's painted bright blue and yellow. The top is finished with jagged edges (representing mountain peaks) and adorned with a single eagle feather.

The drummers, singers, and dancers enter, chanting in unison to the steady clicking of sticks on the rims of the drums. The box drummer sits on a chair facing the wooden drum, his back to the audience. He wears a headdress made from a loon's head and wing feathers. Several young male dancers take their places sitting on the floor, facing him. The twelve frame drummers (all men) sit in a single, long row. They are dressed in bright blue qaspaqs.

Most of the women, in vibrant red, sit in three rows behind the drummers. But several younger women stand facing the box drummer, holding long wands tipped with feathers.

When everyone is in place, as the chant continues, the frame drummers begin playing full force, until the box drummer cuts them off with a wildly irregular beat.

In silence, he begins an elaborate series of gestures. He bows forward from the waist, extending his right arm above his head, full length on the floor. The male dancers do the same and the young women extend their feathered wands.

The singers begin a new chant, accompanied by clicks on the drum rims.

Slowly, the box drummer pulls his arm backward. He holds it there for a moment, then brings it forward rapidly, stopping just short of striking the drum. He does this many times, with stylized gestures of great formality. When he finally strikes the drum, in a sudden unison with the frame drums, the sound is stunning. Tears come to my eyes.

As the dance proceeds, the box drummer begins to swing the drum on its rope. As he swings left, the male dancers move to his right, like puppets on a string. He performs an elaborate series of movements with the drum, which the dancers mirror in reverse.

Several minutes into the dance another dancer appears, also wearing a loon headdress. With each drumbeat he hops two-footed, moving around the Box Drum. Gradually he closes the circle, moving closer and closer to the drummer. Suddenly, in a marvelously fluid movement on his backswing, the box drummer hands the heavy mallet to the dancer, who becomes the new drummer. All this happens without missing a beat.

This drumming, chanting, and dancing is not Art. It encompasses what we usually call Art. But it's more than that. This is not Art for Art's sake. It's not social or political commentary. And it's certainly not self-expression. It subsumes all those things into the larger fabric of life—the life of the individual, the life of the community, the life of the land, and the life of the animals and the spirits that inhabit this place.

This is what so many of us have lost in the twentieth century and what we so desperately need and desire in our lives. This is authentic. This has meaning. This is ritual.

Although this is not my culture, I would rather be here at the Messenger Feast in the Barrow High School gymnasium than in any symphony hall, opera house, or church I can imagine.

About 2 a.m. the festival ends with a processional of all the dance groups and a few songs sung and danced by virtually everyone in the space. The sound of a hundred Iñupiat drummers playing in unison is a sound I'll never forget.

FEBRUARY 7

On the morning plane back to Fairbanks, reading the arts section of last Sunday's *New York Times*, I'm struck again by how remote and moribund the "classical" music world seems. Even the term and most of what it implies simply doesn't apply to the music of most of the interesting composers working today. Embraced by the academy, the avant-garde is dead too.

By about 1950 many composers in America had figured this out. But it's taken another fifty years for the full implications to sink in. And by now we can add postmodernism (whatever *that* was supposed to be!) to the casualty list. The media of the cultural establishment will probably be next-to-last to know. The administrators of most symphony orchestras, opera houses, and foundations will be the last. They'll read about it in the paper. But what a relief for composers. We can simply get on with our work.

A dense fog covers the Arctic Coastal Plain. But as we reach the northern foothills, the stark peaks of the Brooks Range rise up, clear in the pink morning light.

FEBRUARY 8

I'm back to work in the studio, feeling energized and inspired from Barrow. It's still cold, but the light on my afternoon walk is exquisite. 50 below tonight.

FEBRUARY 9

Another productive and satisfying day in the studio, working until after midnight. The new piece seems strange and extreme to me. The textures are so lush and amorphous and relentless. But that's exactly what I had hoped to discover. And at this stage in the process the music is leading me wherever it wants to go. I'm just doing my best to follow.

FEBRUARY 10

The cold is slowly dissipating. After two weeks of 40 below and colder, 20 below feels absolutely balmy. The air is softer now. The light is more intense.

The music continues to unfold almost effortlessly. I find myself a bit overwhelmed, even intimidated by it. That's probably a very good sign.

At evening, the progressive shades of blue—slate, indigo, midnight—are breathtaking. The aurora borealis begins dancing. If only I could find the sounds of *those* colors.

FEBRUARY 12

I'm studying Ellsworth Kelly. A couple of years ago, Cindy and I visited the Guggenheim retrospective of his work. The next day, we took in the Jasper Johns exhibition at the Museum of Modern Art. Both shows made strong impressions, but I was overwhelmed by the richly tactile surfaces and the sheer creative fecundity of Johns's work. Although the whole body of Kelly's work was impressive, I wasn't as immediately enamored of individual pieces. By now, though, it seems to me that my own aspirations in music have more in common with Kelly than with Johns.

The big Mondrian exhibit at MOMA several years back also engaged me. Seeing the paintings themselves gave me a completely different reading of Mondrian. In reproductions, his paintings appear hard-edged and hyper-geometrical (without the obvious "painterly touch" of, say, Barnett Newman's surfaces). But "in person" Mondrian's canvases seem so fragile, so awkward, so human. Still, I've still never been able to completely warm up to Mondrian.

With Kelly the obvious differences between the reproduction and the actual painting are only size and fidelity of color. Beyond that, what you see in one is pretty much what you see in the other. There's little of that tactile element that so appeals to me in art and in music. As John Coplans observes, Kelly is more sensory than sensual. Still, I find myself more taken with Kelly than Mondrian. Maybe it's simply that he's more modern, more "American," and more extreme.

Like Kelly's paintings, my new piece emphasizes only color, form, and space. As I read Coplans's book on Kelly, these words leaped off the page at me: "Since color and the canvas shapes are one and the same . . . color itself takes on spatial characteristics. 'Color' becomes both color and space." I imagine at some point I'll work with harder-edged forms and more impassive, uninflected sounds. *Strange and Sacred Noise* is extreme in its geometric formalism. But the sounds themselves are much too rich and complex to be equivalents to Kelly's hard, flat colors. My guess is that I may find those equivalents in large harmonic blocks of electronic sounds. Silence, too, is likely to be a structural element in such music. But that's another world, very different from the one in which I'm currently immersed. While the new piece is rigorously formal, my hope is that it will sound organic, even formless.

FEBRUARY 14

This evening we attended a performance by musicians and dancers from Bali. The gamelan was *Tirta Sari de Peliatan* (modeled on the older *Semar Pegulingan*) — appropriately for Valentine's Day, the gamelan of the love god. My trip to Barrow and tonight's performance have reminded me that too often I think of music only in terms of metaphor or image, forgetting the fundamental role of the body.

The memory of the bright, shimmering sounds of the gamelan warms and brightens the dark, subzero night.

FEBRUARY 16

I'm fascinated with equivalents, those shared resonances between different phenomena: between landscape and mind, culture and ecosystem, painting and music. Color and form, surface and texture, field and gesture: the equivalents between these elements of music and painting continue to fascinate me.

FEBRUARY 17

One of the defining currents of twentieth-century painting was the movement away from the detached viewpoint of perspective and its illusions of receding depth, toward a new emphasis on color and surface. In music there's been a parallel movement away from the sequential development of relationships between sounds, to a new emphasis on the inherent qualities of sounds heard in the present moment.

Now, at the end of the century, Schoenberg's "atonality" seems to have been a dead end. The far more radical change in Western music was the fundamental shift (beginning with Debussy and Stravinsky, and continuing on through Varèse, Cage, and Nancarrow) from the primacy of Pitch to the primacy of Sound and Time. In this new context, Harmony becomes simply (in Cage's all-encompassing definition) "Sounds heard together."

FEBRUARY 20

What a joy it is to listen with curiosity and fascination as this strange music unfolds, each new sonority emerging from the last. The experience of working on a piece of this scale is like taking a journey through large, open country. I hope the experience of hearing it will be even more absorbing. I want this music to be a wilderness. And I want to get hopelessly lost in it.

FEBRUARY 21–MARCH 4

We're moving into late winter. It's still quite cold, but the light is back, and we're gaining seven minutes each day. The arc of the sun is higher and wider. It no longer sets behind Ester Dome, but farther to the west and north, behind the ridges of Murphy Dome.

For several nights, in early evening, Venus and Jupiter were so close to one another they seemed to be dancing. A week later they've drifted far apart.

Three days of soft snow falling and dusty grey light are followed by several days of sparkling blue. Driving home from the Festival of Native Arts in the wee hours, the aurora is so beautiful I have to whoop out loud.

The animals are more active. The squirrel at the studio has emerged again. The redpolls have joined the chickadees at the feeder. The ravens seem to be more extravagant in flight, and even more vocal than usual. The boreal owl has been calling since late

January. And tonight I hear the great horned owl for the first time this year. Walking through the woods one afternoon last week, I flushed a snowshoe hare—a sudden apparition of white on white.

I feel fortunate to have wild animals as my neighbors.

MARCH 8

I'm back at work on the new piece, moving into the home stretch. I want the sound to be lush and transparent at the same time. The danger is that all the colors will run together.

The physical space, the distance between the instrumental choirs, is an integral part of this music. But I also hope to find a full and purely musical space, in which each of the layers of time, harmony, and timbre is distinctly audible. The diatonic ("white") layers can be lush. But the chromatics should be more transparent—like veils of color floating over the surface. As the manuscript nears completion, I'm thinning out the chromatic layers and re-spacing the harmonies as widely as possible.

MARCH 13

Time has turned into Space and there will be no more Time.
—Samuel Beckett

It's finished, this evening: *The Immeasurable Space of Tones.* Seventy-four minutes of continuous orchestral sound, it's the strangest thing yet to come out of my studio. After six weeks thinking and sketching, actually writing the notes took only about the same amount of time. The piece really did seem to write itself. I'm exhilarated and exhausted.

Twelve years ago, after the première of *The Far Country of Sleep,* my friend Leif Thompson made a prophetic observation: "I especially like that middle section," he said. "You know—the part where nothing happens. That's what you *really* want to do, isn't it?"

I've been trying to find the courage to do this ever since. My fear has been that by leaving everything out of the music there'd be nothing left. Now that I've finally taken the leap and left everything out, my hope is that the only thing left is — the music!

Working on *Immeasurable Space*, I was continually amazed at how much is happening in the music all the time. What at first I thought was static and empty turns out to be remarkably dynamic, full, and constantly changing.

We travel into new territory and slowly we begin to locate ourselves, to understand where we are.

About John Cage

Along with Henry Cowell's *New Musical Resources* and Harry Partch's *Genesis of a Music*, John Cage's *Silence* was one of the books that changed my musical life. When I first read it at the tender age of seventeen, it opened my ears and my mind to a vast new horizon of possibilities. After *Silence* I could never turn back. Thirty years later, Cage's challenge to constantly question our intentions and to remain open to "no matter what eventuality" is still a touchstone for my life and work.

Meeting Cage had a similarly profound impact on me. Each of the several conversations I had with him, in person and over the telephone, taught me valuable lessons—not only about music, but about life. Cage's gentle humor and expansive spirit offered a strong model of how to live as an artist, with honesty, dignity, and grace.

I grew up playing drums in rock 'n' roll bands. But as I began to aspire to becoming a composer of "art" music, I was inclined to renounce my percussive roots. Discovering Cage's percussion music of the 30s and 40s was a real liberation for me. Even more than Varèse, Cage (along with Cowell, Partch, and Lou Harrison) showed me that it was possible to compose complex and sophisticated music for percussion—smart music that also rocked.

As I began to study Cage's percussion pieces composed in his "square root form" (in which rhythm is the same at all levels, from micro to macro), I began to understand the fuller implication of his approach: that Time rather than Harmony could be the primary dimension of musical structure and form. This influence is most obvious in my own works for percussion, such as *Strange and Sacred Noise* and the *Three Drum Quartets from Earth and the Great*

As background for an article he was writing, Kyle Gann asked a group of composers to tell him about the influence that John Cage had on their lives and music. This was my reply.

Weather. But in some measure it's present in virtually everything I do.

Another of Cage's ideas that had a lasting influence on my own work was his concept of a fixed "gamut" of tones and timbres as the harmonic foundation of a piece. This idea grew out of his early percussion and prepared-piano works and reached its peak with the *String Quartet in Four Parts* and *Six Melodies for Violin and Keyboard*. It offered composers a colorful alternative to the charcoal gray of twelve-tone and serial thinking about melody, harmony, and orchestration. Combining it with time-based formal structures, I've developed my own variations on the gamut idea in large-scale orchestral works such as *Clouds of Forgetting, Clouds of Unknowing* and *In the White Silence.*

One of the most far-reaching assertions of Cage's work was the notion (still considered "radical" in some quarters) that music depends on listening. When we listen, the whole world becomes music. After Cage, Western music would never be the same. The center of music is no longer the omniscient composer. It's the listener. And the composer is now free to be a listener too. The broader implications of this musical worldview are ecological. Cage taught us that music is Nature and Nature is music. Over the years, as my own obsession with metaphors from the natural world has become deeper and less overt, I find myself returning again and again to Cage's aspiration "to imitate Nature in her manner of operation."

Dream Paths Crossing

My friend the photographer Wilbur Mills and I were camped on the banks of the Jago River, near its headwaters in the northern foothills of the Brooks Range. It was early June and we were trapped in our small tent while an Arctic spring blizzard howled.

During three days of icy wind and heavy, driving snow we hardly left our sleeping bags. In the cold air and flat gray light, the line between waking and dreaming became blurred. I was haunted by recurring visions of a large brown bear, stalking me across the open tundra.

Near midnight on the third day, the weather broke and we emerged. Before the storm the river had been raging with spring-melt water. Now it had frozen to a trickle. We crossed to the other side and began climbing. Halfway up the slope we came on a small basin full of grass tussocks, covered with new snow and bathed in warm, golden light. Wilbur set up his tripod and began to work.

I continued, hiking to the crest of the ridge where I hoped to look across the coastal plain and catch a glimpse of the Arctic Ocean. At last I reached the ridgeline and a large stone outcrop. Carefully placing my steps over the wet, snowy rocks, I climbed to the top. The view beyond was more breathtaking than I had imagined. The vast Arctic plain swept east and west to the horizons and fifty miles north to the coast, where the midnight sun hung suspended between a brooding, leaden sky and the luminous pack ice of the Beaufort Sea. I stood motionless, transfixed.

Suddenly I was seized by a strange and vivid sense that I was not alone. I felt the powerful presence of another. The hair stood up on the back of my neck. Then it passed.

I don't know how long I stood there, frozen in the beauty of the place and the moment. Eventually I bowed, turned, and began to climb slowly down the rocks, back the way I had come.

Near the bottom of the outcrop I stopped, startled. There, crossing my bootprints in the snow, were the fresh tracks of a large grizzly bear. While I'd been standing no more than thirty feet above, the bear had crossed my path! His trail descended in a broad arc, disappearing down toward the river.

That evening I slept without dreaming. The next afternoon I saw him.

We were sitting in camp when he appeared on a gravel bar a couple of hundred yards upstream. Wilbur grabbed his camera and we moved cautiously in the bear's direction. At what we judged to be a safe distance we sat down in the bushes and Wilbur began photographing.

The bear, a strapping young male, was ripping up willows looking for ground squirrels. It was very early in the season and he was clearly hungry after a long hibernation. Even so, the bear looked healthy. His coat was shiny and we watched in awe as he made his way through the thicket, churning up vegetation and tundra like a bulldozer.

Gradually the bear moved in our direction, and we retreated back to camp. But he kept coming our way. When he emerged from the willows just above our tent, Wilbur and I started talking to him.

"Hey, Brother Bear. Great country you have here. We're just passing through. We won't be here long."

He walked on toward us.

"Hey, now. We don't want any trouble. There's plenty of room out here for all of us."

Wilbur kept photographing. I picked up the borrowed rifle we had with us.

The bear kept coming.

We had no place to go. The river was at our backs. And there were no trees to climb.

About thirty feet away, the bear stopped. He sat up on his hind legs and sniffed the air. He dropped back down on all fours and walked around in a tight circle.

I raised the rifle to my shoulder. But I was trembling so hard that even if I'd been able to bring myself to pull the trigger, I might have missed. Besides, the .30-30 was too small for the job, and an angry wounded bear would be a worst-case scenario. I lowered the gun.

The bear sat up again. He snapped his jaws, growled, and made a short bluff charge in our direction.

Wilbur stopped photographing, and we edged back toward the river.

As we did a strong gust of wind rose up, carrying our scent directly to the bear. He turned and galloped off across the tundra. We watched until he disappeared over a high ridge.

Tools

One summer I was one of five young composers on a concert at the Cabrillo Festival. After the concert there was a panel discussion. At the beginning of the discussion Lou Harrison observed that of the five new works he had heard on the concert, only two had what he called "musical continuity". The other three were composed in what Lou called "video continuity". They were, he said, clearly the work of composers who had grown up with the jump-cuts and rapid-fire pacing of television.

The discussion moved on to a wide range of other topics. Finally, near the end of the session, a member of the audience asked: "How many of you composers whose music we heard today use MIDI and computers in the process of composing your music?" Three hands were raised.

Although no one made explicit the connection with Lou's earlier comment, the point was crystal clear: The tools influence the work.

Inherently most tools are neither good nor bad. But I always try to be aware of the subtle and profound ways in which the tools I use shape the music I make.

In the decade since that little epiphany at Cabrillo, I've gradually integrated the computer into my work process. Initially I used it for notation. Since I'm an inveterate reviser, the appeal of making revisions to a work without the necessity of recopying a new score and performance parts proved irresistible. A year or two later I began using a computer for editing and mixing. This allowed me to produce the CD of *Earth and the Great Weather* in my own studio. A few years after that, I bought a sampler and began using the computer to make demo recordings of new works. And finally, a couple years ago, I bought a laptop computer and began using it as an integral part of my composing.

For a recent revival of *Coyote Builds North America* I decided to make some corrections and minor changes to the score and parts. *Coyote* predates my use of computers, and since I had neither the time nor the money to make or hire the preparation of new electronic editions of the music, I decided to do the job by hand. Looking over the old score and parts, I was immediately struck by the distinctive character of the handwritten calligraphy, the literal trace of the composer's hand. Although I still often make a pencil manuscript from which the electronic score and parts are prepared, it had been many years since I'd copied music in ink. I dug out my elegant old calligraphy pens, but despite my best efforts I couldn't resurrect them. So I did the job with a very inelegant felt-tip pen. The visible discrepancy between the original manuscript and the new additions reminded me of the centrality of notation.

Computers make it easy to compose by playing and recording (in sound or notation), then editing the result. But I still begin with notation. The musical implications of this simple matter are profound. Notation puts a certain distance between the composer and the music. It demands a degree of detachment and abstract thought that I find liberating. Notation frees me from my technical limitations as a performer. It imposes a discipline on my imagination. And notation also allows me to work with forms and patterns that might initially seem "unmusical." But the limitations of traditional musical notation can also inhibit discoveries. The graphic representations of digital audio and sequencing programs constitute a different kind of notation, with different limitations and different possibilities for discovery.

The most exciting potential of computers is the integration of composition, notation, and performance in a single instrument.

What matters most, of course, is the sound of the music. And the problem with much computer music is that it's too much computer and too little music. The tools predominate and the sound is secondary. But when the ear comes first, computers can be powerful tools for both composition and sounding music.

Acquired Tastes

It was the mid-1980s and I was visiting San Francisco. Glenn Branca and his ensemble were also in town. I'd heard a little about Glenn and his notorious symphonies for electric guitars, but I'd never heard the music.

I grew up playing in garage bands, so amplified music was nothing new for me. And I knew enough to bring earplugs to the concert. But even wearing plugs, the sound was ear-splitting, teeth-gnashing, lung-rattling loud. Beyond the sheer decibel level, it seemed there was something unusually brutal and unnerving about this music. It literally pressed me to the floor in a raging storm of dense harmonic waves.

By intermission I was seething. I couldn't speak to my friends in the lobby. Pacing angrily back and forth, I remembered John Cage's similar reaction to a performance by Branca. Cage had left that concert, speaking uncharacteristically harsh words about the music. I made up my mind that come hell and higher volume levels I'd stick this one out. I returned to the hall and submitted to the second half of the concert. At the end I left without speaking to anyone, feeling completely exhausted.

All night long Branca's music continued to reverberate in my body and my mind. By the time I woke up the next morning, I loved it! At first I couldn't quite articulate why. But then it dawned on me that any music capable of eliciting such a strong reaction was worthy of attention. I've been an admirer of Branca's work ever since. And I now make a special point of seeking out music I think I don't like.

Off the Grid, Out of the Box (2000)

Like the streets of midtown Manhattan, the twelve tones of equal temperament were conceived as an idealized grid in which everything is evenly balanced and self-contained. But straight lines and equal increments are rare in nature. And the recent return of non-tempered tunings has opened exciting new possibilities for moving Western music off the grid and out of the box.

In equal temperament, all pitches are theoretically alike. So it's easy to treat them as abstract entities ("notes" rather than tones) and to lose touch with their sounding reality. By contrast, in tunings based on the whole-number relationships of the harmonic series each pitch and each interval has its own unique identity.

In his insightful *Music Primer* Lou Harrison observes that Schoenberg's excellent ear led him to understand that in equal-temperament there is no real "tonality," since all the intervals (except the octave) are untrue. In this light it's not too hard to imagine Schoenberg's twelve-tone technique as the musical equivalent of gridlock. Rather than sit stalled in a dodecaphonic traffic jam, American composers since Harry Partch (many of whom have felt less of an investment than our European counterparts in equal temperament) have chosen to retune. The possibilities for working with different tunings are almost limitless. In my own music I've explored a variety of approaches.

Dream in White on White is one of several of my pieces that can be performed in an acoustically perfect tuning or in equal temperament. This piece was originally scored for harp, string quartet, and string orchestra. The harp is tuned to Pythagorean diatonic intonation, which the string players match by ear. How-

Earlier versions of this essay first appeared in the *Anchorage Daily News* and *NewMusicBox*

ever I've also endorsed performances using piano instead of harp. Of course a piano can be tuned in Pythagorean intervals. When I was composing *Dream*, I retuned the piano in my studio. But in most cases this isn't likely to happen. So the result is essentially an equal-tempered "arrangement" of the piece—the same music with a different set of harmonic and instrumental colors.

The music for strings in my opera *Earth and the Great Weather* embraces intervals up to the 105th harmonic. This is done by retuning the open strings of the instruments to the first eight odd-numbered harmonics of the low D on the double bass. Virtually all the sounds in the piece are either open strings or natural harmonics, so the problem of finding the correct pitch is minimized. But since the open strings are retuned, the violin, viola, cello, and bass essentially become transposing instruments. The sounds the players expect from a given fingering are definitely *not* the sounds that they hear. To deal with this I employ a notation that shows the string (with a Roman numeral), the harmonic (with an Arabic numeral), and the sounding pitch. (The higher the harmonic, the more approximate the note names become. But I chose not to show the precise deviation from equal temperament, since most of the pitches are natural harmonics and the players don't have to adjust them by ear.)

When the musicians in my ensemble were first learning to hear and play in this harmonic world they tuned their open strings by ear, following the ascending harmonics of the bass. This process could take as long as an hour. So for later performances we used a computer-generated tape. All this may sound complicated, but the tuning and the notation in *Earth and the Great Weather* turned out to be thoroughly practical for performance.

After several years working with non-tempered tunings, I returned to twelve-tone equal temperament in *Clouds of Forgetting, Clouds of Unknowing*—an hour-long piece for chamber orchestra. *Clouds* follows a rigorously formal course through the expanding

From Earth and the Great Weather

intervals of the chromatic scale, through which I hoped to discover for myself a new palette of chords, "modes," and harmonic colors.

After *Clouds* came *Strange and Sacred Noise*—an extended cycle of pieces for percussion quartet. As the title suggests, this piece is a celebration of noise, composed almost entirely of non-pitched sounds. In the one piece of the *Noise* cycle that is scored for tuned instruments (marimbas, vibraphones, and crotales) I treated twelve-tone equal temperament quite literally as a grid, superimposing a quadrilateral fractal (the Sierpinski carpet) onto the chromatic field to derive the clouds and clusters of the music.

Twelve-tone equal temperament is just one among a whole world of tonal resources available to composers today. And there's no good reason (musical or technical) that we shouldn't explore as many of these as we choose.

If tunings grounded in the harmonic series can lead music off the grid of equal temperament and out into new and open country, what are the possibilities in the field of rhythm?

Most Western music continues to display a curious two-dimensionality of time. The bar lines delineate little boxes containing precisely measured portions of time. Even when the rhythms within those boxes are relatively complex, they're still usually bouncing off the measured walls that contain them.

Stravinsky railed against the tyranny of the bar line. By rapidly juxtaposing boxes of different dimensions—measures of different meters—he created a new illusion of depth on a regular temporal plane, much as Picasso and Braque did with Cubist painting. Charles Ives was a pioneer of multi-dimensional musical space. Although still fundamentally narrative and pictorial in conception, his dense, multi-layered music began to move beyond the "story-without-words" theatrical space of Berlioz and Strauss, toward an enveloping temporal and physical space in which events occur more like those in nature. Edgard Varèse shut the storybook completely, constructing like an architect in an abstract geometry of sound.

Returning to the harmonic series as the foundation of theory and practice, Henry Cowell in his visionary book *New Musical Resources* (1919/1930) proposed a unified field theory of musical time. As Cowell observed, pitch is simply fast rhythm. And rhythm is merely slow pitch. In his *Quartet Romantic* (1915–17) and several other works, Cowell attempted to achieve a formal convergence of pitch and rhythm.

Cowell's postulation of rhythms derived from the ratios of the harmonic series inspired Conlon Nancarrow to explore unprecedented rhythmic and tempo relationships in his extraordinary works for player piano. Nancarrow rigorously and thrillingly expanded the possibilities of musical time. As he sustained multiple tempo layers throughout entire compositions, a rich new temporal depth opened up for Western music.

Also inspired by Cowell, Lou Harrison (who is best known for his lyrical music in just intonation) translated the ratios of just intonation into rhythmic terms in his *Fugue for Percussion* (1942). In several of his most radical works, Harrison stepped outside even that most widely accepted harmonic enclosure—the octave. In the *Simfony in Free Style* (1955) and *At the Tomb of Charles Ives* (1966), all the tones are tuned by whole-number ratios, which move from pitch to pitch without regard for the limits of the octave. Lou calls this type of intonation "free style." Might a similar unbounded style be applied to rhythmic and temporal relationships that step completely outside the box of the recurring bar line?

Composers now have powerful new tools that make it far easier to achieve precision and flexibility in both harmony and rhythm. Personal computers offer the power to create music in Harrison's "free style" without the need for cumbersome re-tuning of fixed-pitch instruments and without unrealistic amounts of rehearsal. We can use electronics and computers to create finished pieces.

We can use them to create electronic demos to help us learn to hear and play new relationships. And the same tools we can use for tuning can be applied to rhythm, tempo, and duration.

The time seems right to follow the harmonic series off the grid and out of the box.

Digital Revelation

It must have been 1993. Jay Cloidt and I were at work in my little wood-burning studio, preparing the master tape for the CD of *Earth and the Great Weather*. The various musical elements — strings, voices, drums, natural sounds — had been recorded as separate tracks, which we were laboriously editing, processing, and layering into an elaborate mix on the computer.

Several days into the project we were lost in a blizzard of technical difficulties. Everything was going wrong and there seemed to be no glimmer of hope. Finally when the computer froze for the ninth or tenth time, I pushed back my chair and threw up my hands in frustration.

"This is ridiculous!" I complained. "All this technology and none of it works! The next thing you know, I'll be making *electronic* music!"

Jay took a beat. He grinned a wry little grin, looked me straight in the eye, and spoke softly, with mock sensitivity: "Well, John. What do you think *this* is?"

Farthest North Mountains
Arctic National Wildlife Refuge (1999)

We take off from Fairbanks and fly north, over the familiar landmarks of home—Ester Dome, Moose Mountain, Murphy Dome, Gilmore Dome—and on across the White Mountains, Beaver Creek, Birch Creek, and the Yukon Flats—that vast labyrinth of lakes, ponds, muskegs, oxbows, and sinuous stream courses. Crossing the great river at Fort Yukon, we continue on up the Christian River, across the hills and forests of the northern interior to Arctic Village. As our Navajo approaches from the south, we see a Cessna touching down from the north. It's our friend and favorite bush pilot, Don Ross, right on schedule.

Don was our pilot ten years ago this week when Cindy and I had our wedding in the Arctic Refuge. This is our anniversary trip. We're celebrating ten years of marriage and twenty years as a couple. In the company of our good friends, the conductor Gordon Wright and the photographer Dennis Keeley, we're hoping to return to the site of our wedding: Okpilak Lake on the Okpilak River, which flows north out of the Brooks Range and into the Arctic Ocean. We exchange greetings with Don as we load our gear from one plane and into the other. Within minutes we're in the air again. Don will drop Dennis and me off almost a hundred miles to the north, then return to shuttle Cindy and Gordon.

As we climb steeply, up the East Fork of the Chandalar River and into the Brooks Range, I feel as though I'm coming home. We pass over Red Sheep Creek, the starting point of a trip we made in 1981. From the air I can retrace our route for that entire trip—a loop hike up Red Sheep, over a low pass, and down Cane Creek, followed by a float down the East Fork back to Arctic Village.

Don picks his way around the clouds that have piled up over the crest of the mountains. We slip over the Arctic Divide and down into the headwaters of the Hulahula River. The slopes below are laced with caribou trails and we see small groups of Dall sheep here and there. To the west I can see Mount Michelson and the un-named peak in the Franklin Mountains that I climbed as a young man, twenty-two years ago. I remember floating the Kongakut River, farther to the east, later that same summer. And the trip into the upper Jago River in 1981, when a friend and I were caught for three days in a spring blizzard and had a memorable en-counter with a grizzly bear. These and other trips have mythic sig-nificance in my life. For me this is sacred ground, the holy land. It's also the country from which *Earth and the Great Weather* was born. The Gwich'in and Iñupiaq names for places in this geogra-phy formed the *Arctic Litanies* of that piece. As we fly over the land, the sounds of those names and the music they inspired resonate in my mind's ear.

Farther downstream, as the country begins to flatten out, Don turns east and crosses over into the Okpilak River valley. As he circles low around Okpilak Lake, I see our wedding campsite and the hill where the ceremony took place. But the tundra looks too wet for a safe landing, so we turn west and fly back over the Hula-hula and into the Sadlerochit Mountains, an area I've wanted to visit for many years. The Sadlerochits are the farthest north mountains in Alaska, a relatively small and low range jutting out onto the Arctic Coastal Plain, separate from the main mass of the Brooks Range.

Don touches down on a tundra bench beside Itkilyariak Creek. We quickly unload the gear and he takes off again, back to Arc-tic for Cindy and Gordon. Dennis and I sit back and bask in the country for a while, then begin to set up camp. By the time we hear Don's plane again (a couple of hours later), we've pitched our tents, found drinking water, established a kitchen on a gravel bar in the creek, and set up a community shelter on the bank.

We greet Cindy and Gordon, and unload their gear. To the north, a dense fog is rolling in off the ice of the Beaufort Sea. Don needs to fly out to the coast before the fog settles in, so he can shuttle a group out from Camden Bay tomorrow morning. But he decides to stay and have dinner with us. With everyone's assistance, Cindy whips up a gourmet meal. As we're dining she spots a large male grizzly not far beyond the plane. We watch intently as the bear roots around for a while, then disappears over the bank and into the creek bed.

After dinner, as Don takes off, the bear charges up the opposite bank of the creek and lights out across the tundra. We watch him for quite a while until he disappears into the willows a mile or so up a side stream. We know he's now some distance away. Still, his presence lingers.

Although we would've loved to return to the Okpilak, we're thrilled to be here.

JUNE 25

We rise to a beautiful clear day. The sun is warm and the air pleasantly cool. There's just enough of a down-valley breeze to keep the mosquitoes suppressed. We settle into camp—finding the best waterhole, gathering bits of dry willow for firewood, soaking up the country and surveying the enticing hiking options. This is a magical spot. This valley runs north and south, joining the crest of the Brooks Range with the Arctic coast. Looking south we have a full view of Mount Chamberlin, at nine thousand feet the highest peak in the Brooks. Looking north we see out across the coastal plain to Camden Bay and the ice of the Beaufort Sea.

Later in the day we hike downstream to the mouth of the valley and out onto the edge of the coastal plain. Deeply worn, ancient-looking caribou trails follow the course of Itkilyariak Creek. Historically, this must be a major route for the annual migration of the Porcupine River herd. We climb a high ridge, hoping to catch sight of the caribou. This is the time of aggregation. After giving birth to their calves, the caribou gather together in the tens of thousands out on the coastal plain to begin their migration east into the Yukon Territory. We see no caribou today. But the view across the great plain is endless and breathtaking.

After dinner we're sitting around talking quietly when an Arctic fox walks brazenly into camp. We fall silent. The fox advances, sniffing here and there. He stops not twenty feet away, looks us over intently, and then continues on downstream.

JUNE 26

This morning Cindy and Gordon head off for a hike across a major valley on the other side of the creek. Dennis and I stay behind to make recordings of the small Aeolian harp I've brought with me. (The same harp that provided the music for the wedding ceremony on the Okpilak, ten years ago.) I sit on a mossy outcropping, amid flowering avens and rhododendron, basking in this place while tuning the forty nylon strings of the harp. Dennis is happily photographing the microenvironments of the tundra and the macro-environment of the mountains. At last I achieve an acceptable unison on the harp and we begin recording.

The conditions are perfect. It's warm and sunny. And the omnipresent down-valley breeze translates into no bugs and lots of music from the harp. After a while the power supply for the microphone begins to act up. I attempt a repair but soon realize that I feel relieved that the equipment isn't working. So I decide to give it up. I don't really need to make these recordings. I need to be fully present in this place. I pack up the recording gear, turn to Dennis and say: "Let's go climbing." Quite innocently he replies, "OK!" And we set out up the creek above camp.

Photo by Dennis Keeley

Something happens to me when I get into the mountains. My body is now middle-aged, but my mind suddenly thinks I'm a kid again. Poor Dennis! I don't think he's ever been on a hike like this. The canyon gets progressively steeper, and there are numerous false summits. At each one I wait for Dennis, shouting words of encouragement back downhill. When he arrives we share a quick snack or a drink of water and survey the surroundings. Then I charge on ahead. I tell myself that I'm doing this to find the best route and save Dennis wasted energy. The truth is, I can't contain my excitement. I'm sure Dennis knows this. Fortunately he's a true friend and a real trooper.

After a couple of hours of arduous climbing, we finally arrive in a breathtaking alpine bowl. Far below to the northeast, we can make out large patches of overflow ice on the Sadelrochit River. Surrounded by snow, we lie on the naked stone and listen to a gorgeous antiphonal duet by two Lapland longspurs accompanied by the mountain wind. This is the music of heaven.

JUNE 27

This morning we lounge around camp. Dennis photographs. Cindy reads and scans for animals. Gordon stretches out with a book of crossword puzzles, which he does the same way Morton Feldman composed—not in pencil, but directly in ink! This is true mastery. I set up a makeshift writing table and begin work (in pencil) on a new piece for an ensemble in Japan. After a few hours of composing I'm up for a hike. So is everyone else.

We cross the creek and head off across the tundra on the other side, roughly following the path of the bear we saw on our first evening here. We reach the last mountain before the coastal plain. Cindy and Gordon want to follow the small creek upstream. Dennis and I decide to climb. This is a steeper and more rugged ascent than the one we made yesterday. But it's shorter too. Within an hour or so we're standing on top, looking out across the coastal plain and the sea beyond.

It's been ten years since I've seen this stretch of coast. As I trace the Canning River down to its delta, my heart sinks. Just beyond the mouth of the river is an enormous drilling platform. Although I knew about the offshore leases in the Beaufort Sea, I'd put them out of mind. This brings it all home in an undeniable form. The structure is thirty miles in the distance, but it looms large and ominous on the horizon. Is this a symbol of things to come?

Since my first trip on the Canning in 1977, some things have changed. In 1980 the Alaska National Interest Lands Conservation Act doubled the size of the Arctic National Wildlife Range and renamed it the Arctic National Wildlife Refuge. The Act also granted Wilderness protection to the mountains of the Refuge. The small role I played in that effort remains one of the most deeply satisfying experiences of my life.

But some things have stayed the same. Although Jimmy Carter was a strong advocate of protecting Alaska's wildlands, after Ronald Reagan was elected the Alaska Lands Act was passed hurriedly with several glaring defects. Among these was the lack of protection for the coastal plain of the Arctic Refuge. Two decades later oil drilling remains an imminent threat. This monumental drilling rig just outside the boundary of the refuge is an undeniable reminder of that threat.

Dennis and I descend quickly to find Cindy and Gordon waiting, right where we left them. As we make our way back toward camp we spot a band of musk oxen a mile or so away on the edge of the plain. There are about twenty animals, including several calves. Awkward in appearance but graceful in movement, musk oxen have a prehistoric air about them. Their presence here reassures us that the ancient rhythms of this place are still complete. We watch them for a long time, wondering what the future will bring for the musk oxen, the caribou, and all the other animals that live here.

At dinner we watch as a dense blanket of fog rolls in off the sea ice and advances rapidly across the plain, coming our way.

JUNE 28

We wake to dense fog and icy wind blowing off the Arctic Ocean. The mountains have vanished. Pools in the creek and puddles in the tundra are covered with half an inch of new ice. The windblown fog races upstream, like a dry-ice and wind-machine scene on a 1930s movie set.

After breakfast we stand around wondering what to do. We're wearing all the clothes we have with us and still we're cold. The visibility is too low for us to hike anywhere. So we head back to our tents, where we spend most of the day. Periodically we drift back to the kitchen, to talk, eat, and sip hot drinks before returning to the warmth of our sleeping bags.

Cindy and I reminisce about our wedding and things that have happened in our lives in the decade since. We've always had a passionate relationship. In the summer of 1989, after ten stormy years, we found ourselves at the moment of truth. We'd talked about marriage for a long time. But our pattern was that when one of us was ready, the other wasn't. Then the roles would switch. After doing this little dance for far too long, something had to change. We had either to give it up or take it to the next level.

That June Cindy and our friend Debbie Miller were camped along with their kids by the Okpilak River ("The River with No Willows"). My friend Leif Thompson and I flew in to spend a few days before taking off on a hike into the mountains.

As I unloaded my pack from the plane Cindy smiled at me and asked in her most offhand tone: "So . . . You wanna get married?"

Mustering all the nonchalance I could, I replied, "Sure."

Debbie and our pilot Don Ross heard the exchange. So we had witnesses and the deal was sealed. A few days later Debbie's husband Dennis, who was flying surveys of the Porcupine caribou herd, dropped in with a wedding cake and a couple of bottles of champagne imported from Fairbanks.

Because it's sometimes a long way to the justice of the peace, Alaska law allows ordinary citizens to be appointed as marriage commissioners to officiate at wedding ceremonies. (I've had the honor of doing this myself for two other couples.) So Debbie officiated at our wedding. Leif was the photographer. Debbie's three-year-old daughter Robin was Cindy's maid of honor. Our son Sage served as a combination of best man and father of the bride, giving us away to one another.

Cindy and I spent most of our wedding day writing our vows. Debbie also wrote her statement for the ceremony. Sage and his friend Seth gathered tundra flowers and (with Debbie's guidance) fashioned two lovely garlands that Cindy and I wore in our hair. I had brought with me a small Aeolian harp that I tuned to a special mode for the occasion. The harp would be our organ and the wind would be the organist.

The boys had tied colorful bandanas to willow sticks to make wedding banners. With one of these Sage led the procession. Behind him was Debbie, with her newborn daughter Casey strapped to her chest. Cindy was next, the loveliest of brides—wearing knee-high, black rubber tundra boots and a blue wool kaspaq. I followed, carrying Robin in a backpack and the wind harp on my head. And Seth, flying his banner, was the tail of the procession. Leif circled in and out, documenting the event for our faraway friends and family.

We hiked across a small creek, over the tundra and up a hill at the north end of the valley. There, with Sage standing between us holding tight to both our arms, Cindy and I exchanged our vows. Leif raised a kite on the wind. The music of the harp floated across the tundra.

No one had a watch. So to this day we still don't know whether we were married on June 30 or July 1. But the sun was low in the north and everything was bathed in deep golden evening light.

We strolled back down to camp, where we ate wedding cake, drank champagne, and danced around a fire we built on a gravel bar in the river. The sun disappeared behind the ridge. We put the kids to bed, returned to the fire, and began telling stories.

Suddenly something caught my ear. I ran up the riverbank to get away from the sound of the water. Cindy, Leif, and Debbie followed. There, on the very spot where we had spoken our vows, sat a lone wolf, howling to the sky. Above the wolf, a pair of snowy owls circled on the cool air.

The wolf howled again.

I looked at Cindy. She looked at me, smiled sweetly, and said: "Go."

At that moment, we both knew our marriage would last.

We embraced and kissed. Then I headed out across the tundra.

Ten years later, here we are again. I decide to take advantage of this day in the tent to get some serious work done on the new piece. Although this is definitely not the weather we've been hoping for, it's fine for one day. (This is, after all, the Arctic.) But we've been stormbound too many times in the past, and we know that a front like this could set in for days on end. The clouds and the fog are so dense that it almost gets dark tonight. We fall asleep hoping for the best.

In the middle of the night I wake up to silence. The wind has stopped, so I crawl out of the tent to check the sky. The fog has retreated halfway across the coastal plain. The slopes between here and there are bathed in warm golden light.

JUNE 29

By the time I rise again the morning is brilliant. The warm, gentle breeze has returned, blowing downstream from the mountains to the south. This is a good sign. We decide to make a day-long hike up the valley to Sunset Pass. We set out toward the looming form of Mount Chamberlin. The grade is gentle and the footing on the gravel bars and creek banks is good. In little time we're out of sight of camp. All along the creek, on both sides, caribou trails are carved deep into the tundra.

As the valley narrows we see ahead an unusual number of white spots against the green-brown of the land. Soon we come on a circle of stones about twelve feet in diameter. It's a tent ring! Judging from the depth to which the stones have sunk into the tundra and the amount of lichen growing on them, this is an ancient site. Although we know better, until this moment we could almost imagine that we are the first people in this place. Now, in an instant, ten thousand years of human history come to life. We can imagine skin tents weighted down around the edges with these white stones, and person-sized stone cairns placed here and there to funnel the caribou into this narrow spot where the people could hunt them easily. The people could have been the Iñupiat from the coast or the Gwich'in from the forest to the south. Historically, the Iñupiat and Gwich'in were enemies. And though we're closer to the coast than to we are to the forest, this low pass and north-south valley create an easy route by which the Gwich'in came north in search of the caribou. The Iñupiaq name for this creek, Itkilyariak, echoes this. (It translates roughly as "the Indian route.") We see no other people and no caribou. But we feel both as a powerful presence in this place.

Farther on up the valley, we find two more tent rings. The land continues rising in a series of benches, like an enormous flight of stairs to the pass. As we enter the summit area the ground becomes rockier and Mount Chamberlin looms even larger. On the other side are the headwaters of a large creek that flows into the Sadlerochit River, a marshy area spanning the full breadth of the valley. Hiking through this would be wet and arduous. After resting for a while Dennis and Gordon decide to turn back toward camp. Cindy and I head up a side creek that flows from the east, to sit at the base of the mountains. There on a mossy bench, we make love.

JUNE 30

The fine weather continues. After yesterday's hike we decide to take an easy day. Sitting in the sun outside the tent I continue my work on the new music. There are almost no mosquitoes. The hard freeze of two days ago apparently killed them off. But the next wave will be along, soon enough. So we enjoy it while we can.

In mid afternoon we're startled as a single young caribou comes galloping, wild-eyed, down the creek bed and barreling on toward the coast. The look on its face is understandable since the main body of the herd has long since left this part of the country, headed for Canada.

JULY 1

Today is Cindy's and my wedding anniversary. At least we think so. Our wedding ceremony was bathed in that exquisite light that comes when the sun sinks low and begins rolling along the northern horizon over the Arctic Ocean. Although we're still not sure whether we were married late on June 30 or in the first hours of July 1, we settled on the latter, so today's the day. But today as on that day ten years ago, none of us could come close to telling you what time it is. We're doing well enough to know what day it is.

This far north, with the extreme cycles of light and darkness, clock time doesn't make much sense. Out here on the tundra the flow of time itself slows down. On days like these it almost stands still. If only I could achieve something like this in music. The new piece is titled *Time Undisturbed* and the score bears an inscription from Samuel Beckett: "Time has turned into Space and there will be no more time." These words sound a little like something from the Book of Revelation or perhaps quantum physics. But out here the unity of time and space is not apocalyptic, existential, or theoretical. It's physical; a palpable presence that permeates everything—the light, the land, the air.

To celebrate our anniversary we decide to hike up to the dramatic outcroppings at the head of the main tributary of Itkilyariak Creek. Several days ago Cindy and Gordon hiked to the base of these tors. Since then we've been studying them through field glasses from camp and we're all eager to climb among them in that upper basin.

The outcroppings sit on a small plateau that rises suddenly into the high cirque. The climb is slow and steep, but the top is more fantastic than we had imagined. This is one of the most haunting places I've ever been. These stones are like the ruins of some ancient city, a high citadel surrounded by mountains. The formations resemble crumbling buildings, monuments, and statues. There are spirits here. But unlike the human and animal presence we felt in Sunset Pass, the feeling here is older and more primal, from the time before time.

We linger for a couple of hours. Drifting apart, each of us falls into our own reveries. We walk among the outcroppings, climbing those we can, sitting, watching, listening. We wish we'd brought shelter and sleeping bags to spend the night here.

As we approach the northern edge of the plateau, a wild cry pierces the air. We look up to see a northern goshawk descending rapidly toward us. She dives at us several times, screaming constantly. There must be a nest somewhere nearby. So we move away until she relents. Then we stop and sit, watching her through the binoculars. The goshawk never reveals the location of her nest. She is still circling as we begin our descent. None of us wants to leave. We tell ourselves that someday we will return.

On the way back to camp, Gordon and Dennis forge on ahead,

leaving Cindy and me to savor an anniversary stroll. As we get onto more level ground we hold hands while we walk, quietly renewing our vows to one another. I tell Cindy that over these past few days I've felt something I've never experienced before: a deep sense of peace. I've felt contentment and comfort many times in my life. But this is more profound. Maybe it's this place, the fine weather, and the perfect company. Or maybe at last, in midlife, I've begun to discover something like faith.

JULY 2

Today is likely to be our final full day here. The excellent weather holds, so we decide to take a hike far out onto the coastal plain. We follow our creek downstream beyond the edge of the mountains, past the place where we saw the musk oxen, and on. Out on the plain my eyes fall on a large white spot. My heart leaps into my throat: a polar bear! But close inspection through the binoculars reveals only a large snowbank.

We decide to use the snow as a bearing and a destination. At first we guess it's a mile or two away. But after hiking for a long time, the spot seems no closer at all. Out here on the plain there's nothing against which to measure anything—no trees, no mountains or other landmarks to suggest any sense of scale. Immersed in all this undifferentiated space, we've lost all perspective.

I remember once years ago when my friend Leif and I were camped on the plain not far from here. In low light we set out toward a strange outcropping, a white monolith protruding from the tundra an indeterminate distance away. We walked and walked toward that stone, but it never seemed to get any larger. We were stunned when it suddenly rose on sprawling wings and flew away—a snowy owl.

Now Gordon and Cindy have stopped. Dennis and I press on, determined to "get somewhere." I'm watching Dennis ahead of me. As he strides across the tundra his feet are rising and falling at a steady pace. But it appears he's not moving at all. He seems to be walking in place.

Finally we give up. The phantom snowbank seems as far away as ever. Just as I turn to begin the walk back into the mountains, two small flecks of yellow catch my eye. This is not the yellow of mountain avens, cinquefoil, or any flower that blooms here. Something is out of place. As I bend down to investigate I'm startled to find two small strands of wire protruding from the tundra. I try to pull them out, but they won't budge. Then it hits me with full force that these wires and whatever they're attached to in the ground are residue from explosive charges used in seismic testing for oil-bearing formations in the earth. The drilling hasn't begun. But here—just outside the boundary of the officially protected Wilderness and in the very heart of the caribou calving grounds—is yet another potent reminder of the impending threat to this place.

Following Dennis again as we head south, I'm amazed at the difference in my perception. He's walking with the same gait as before. But now he appears to be galloping, almost flying against the backdrop of the mountains.

JULY 3

This morning the air is actually warm. The downstream breeze is barely present and the mosquitoes are back in full force. Reluctantly we break camp, clean up the traces of our presence, and pack our gear. Then we spend several hours wandering around the tundra, storing up the sounds, smells, and images of this place. I'm working on my manuscript when the drone of Don's Cessna breaks the aural horizon. A couple of minutes later we see him, against the backdrop of Mount Chamberlin, flying straight down the valley.

First in, last out: Cindy and Gordon take off with Don, back to Arctic Village. Dennis and I are left exposed as the sun and the bugs grow more intense. After a while we break out the community shelter and seek refuge. Hours go by, but no Don. Heavy clouds have piled up over the mountains and we begin to guess that the weather has trapped him on the other side of the divide. We make dinner and are thinking about setting up camp again when we hear the plane.

As we fly up Itkilyariak Creek I can see all the places we've been these past days. The high cirque, the peak across the creek, the stone tors, even the tent rings in the pass. I would gladly stay here for another couple of weeks.

The flight out is a wild one. The wind is strong. The clouds over the mountains are thick and angry. As we approach the divide, we rise and fall like a roller coaster. Near the crest we're slammed by a fierce downdraft. Even Don looks a bit concerned. He's the best pilot I've ever flown with and I'm confident he has the situation in hand. Still, I'm relieved to finally step out onto the landing strip at Arctic.

Cindy and Gordon have gone. They caught the scheduled flight back to Fairbanks. So it looks like a bivouac for Dennis and me, here at Arctic International. We scout around and finally find a halfway level spot for the tent. We're just finishing dinner when Sarah James pulls up on a four-wheeler. Sarah is one of the most outspoken leaders of the Gwich'in opposition to oil drilling in the Arctic Refuge. I hop onto the back of her machine and we tear off down the dusty road into the village. Sarah drops me at the cabin of our friend Lincoln Tritt.

A former chief of Arctic Village, Lincoln is a writer, a singer, and an outspoken advocate of traditional Gwich'in wisdom and lifeways. He was one of my collaborators on *Earth and the Great Weather*, and it's been at least two years since I've seen him. We pick up right where we left off, talking about everything from the pre-contact culture of his people to oil drilling in the Refuge and global warming. In a little while Sarah returns with Dennis, then takes off again.

After a cup of tea the three of us walk over to the village grave-yard, where many of Lincoln's relatives are buried. I'm struck again by the deep and ancient roots that Lincoln and his people have in this place and by the rapid and traumatic changes they've endured since the coming of Europeans. I don't envy their tur-moil of change. But I do envy the way in which Lincoln and his people belong to this place, and I tell him so.

Dennis makes a portrait of Lincoln and me. We say goodbye and Dennis and I begin our walk back to the airstrip. All around us, from the woods and the ponds that dot the tundra, birds are singing in the midnight light.

Clouds of Forgetting,
Clouds of Unknowing (1996)

Love is most nearly itself
When here and now cease to matter.
—T. S. Eliot

Quantum physics has recently confirmed what shamans and mystics, poets and musicians have long known: the universe is more like music than like matter. It may well be that our most fundamental relationship to the great mysteries is one of listening. Through sustained, concentrated attention to the fullness of the present moment, we listen for the breath of being, the voice of God.

Clouds of Forgetting, Clouds of Unknowing is a work of musical contemplation, an aspiration to consecrate a small time and space for extraordinary listening. The work is titled after *The Cloud of Unknowing*, a fourteenth-century Christian text which has much in common with the teachings of contemplative traditions throughout the world, be they Jewish, Buddhist, Sufi, Native American, or other. The essence of the contemplative experience is voluntary surrender, purposeful immersion in the fullness of a presence far larger than we are.

The Cloud of Unknowing teaches that we can achieve communion only through the Grace of divine Love. To prepare ourselves to receive this gift, we must enter a state of quiet stillness, suspended between heaven and earth. Above—between us and God—lies a "cloud of unknowing" that our understanding can never penetrate. Between ourselves and the world, we must create a "cloud of forgetting," leaving conscious thought and desire below. In this timeless place of forgetting and unknowing, we may begin to hear that for which we are listening.

T. S. Eliot said it this way:

> We must be still and still moving
> Into another intensity
> for a further union, a deeper communion
> Through the dark cold and the empty desolation . . .

John Cage once inquired of a musician trained in the classical traditions of India: "What is the purpose of music?"

Her reply made a profound impression on the composer: "The purpose of music is to quiet the mind, thus rendering it susceptible to divine influences."

Of course music can have many purposes. But in order to quiet the mind we must give up our attachment to that which is "interesting," that which diverts and engages our intellect. We must let crumble the walls of boredom that we build between our awareness and the fullness of each moment.

Cage was fond of saying that if he found something boring for five minutes, he would try it for fifteen. If it were boring for fifteen minutes, he would try it for half an hour. If it were still boring after half an hour, he would try it for an hour, and so on. Sooner of later, he said, we discover that *everything* is interesting. Beyond interest and boredom lie "another intensity" and "a deeper communion."

To find communion we must lose perspective. What, after all, is perspective but a way of removing ourselves from experience?

A painter friend once showed me slides of his paintings from Antarctica. Among these was a view of the Ross Ice Shelf that struck me as one of the most compelling of his images I had seen. The composition is stark in its simplicity. A large field of azure and lavender sky is separated from a lower field of somber purples and coal black by the startling yellow edge of the ice.

Although it occupies the middle ground between the open water and the plateau of ice and sky, that serrated yellow line appears to float—emerging into the foreground only to recede again into the middle ground and the distance. The result is a continual shifting between vertical and horizontal, here and there, near and far.

"What makes this happen?" I wondered. Is it the interrelationships of the shapes? The relative weights and masses of the large color fields? The vivid contrast of the jagged line?

In the same portfolio was another image of the same portion of the Ross Ice Shelf, painted from a vantage point only a few hundred feet away from the first. Despite breathtaking hues, this painting struck me as less effective. Initially I couldn't say why. But my eye kept returning to a rock outcropping in the lower right-hand corner. Finally it occurred to me that this was the crucial difference.

The outcropping defines the foreground. In doing so it fixes the ice edge in the middle distance, freezing its mysterious floating quality at a specific point in space. Because of the outcropping, the second painting projects a more definite sense of the almost incomprehensible scale of the Antarctic landscape. At the same time it removes one from the full presence of the place. The country is so large it seems to disappear, as if viewed through too wide a lens.

The first painting has no definition of foreground. It invites no fixed perspective. By not telling us precisely where we are standing, it invites us to travel freely within the full dimensions of an ambiguous space—from the farthest horizon to a veil of colored mist suspended just before our eyes. This painting is so powerful because it creates a presence that demands our participation. It requires us to explore and discover for ourselves an imaginary space grounded in a remarkable natural landscape. I aspire to a similar experience in music.

In Western music melody and harmony are the equivalents of

figure and ground. Together they constitute a kind of musical perspective, which evolved parallel to that of Renaissance painting. In the musical textures of *Clouds of Forgetting, Clouds of Unknowing* I wanted to lose musical perspective, to blend line and chord into a single sphere of musical space. Clouds of short melodic cells are superimposed on expansive harmonic clouds of the same tones. Figure becomes ground in dense clouds of expanding, rising lines. Ground becomes figure in the glacial movement of large harmonic clouds, which (as the listener enters the suspended time-frame of the music) begin to sound melodic—like exaggeratedly slow chorales.

Near the end of the piece elongated piano arpeggios rise above sustained harmonic clouds in the strings and woodwinds. But the chords are simply echoes of the arpeggios, extending and amplifying the effect of the piano's sustain pedal.

Much of my recent work has explored the natural intervals of the harmonic series, in just intonation and other non-tempered tunings. But *Clouds* is a return to the rich complexities and ambiguities of equal temperament and chromatic modes. This is my most complete and direct statement to date of a personal harmonic idiom that has developed over the course of many years. Formally, the work describes a single, expansive harmonic arch—moving over the course of an hour from unisons and minor seconds, through the succession of equal-tempered intervals, to major sevenths, and finally to the perfect clarity of octaves.

A somewhat unlikely pair of ghosts haunts this music: Morton Feldman and Anton Bruckner. These two have more in common than might first meet the ear.

Bruckner, we are told, was a shy, simple and retiring man of deep Christian faith. In contrast, Feldman was an urbane and outspoken man of strong opinions. Although he joked that he aspired to be "the Jewish Mozart," it's not clear to me what role the practice of Judaism may have played in Feldman's life. But once in conversation, when he complained that most contemporary art-

From Clouds of Forgetting, Clouds of Unknowing

ists seemed to be in some form or other of "show business," I asked him: "What's *your* business?"

After a long, pregnant pause, he replied with a single startling word: "Religion!"

For me, both Bruckner and Feldman are essentially religious composers. Both worked with expansive scales of time and space. Both were romantic idealists who—even at their most passionate and sensuous moments—aspired to transcend self-expression through concentrated images, clarity of sound, breadth and balance of form. Both Feldman and Bruckner created music that is not so much a language of tones as an architecture of sounding images, a sonic sculpture of transcendence.

One of the great powers of music is that it can mean nothing and anything, sometimes at once. Living in Alaska for most of my creative life, I've come to measure my own work and all human creations against the overwhelming presence of the place itself. My music has long been grounded in a strong sense of place and a deep response to the landscapes of the far north, exploring a territory I call "sonic geography." But the landscapes of *Clouds* are more essentially sonic and geometric than geographic in nature.

In this work I wanted not to compose a *piece* of music, but to create a *wholeness* of music with no extra-musical references—a sonic presence somehow equivalent to that of a vast landscape. Still (perhaps unavoidably for me), the sound of this music has a certain coldness, clarity, aridity, and starkness reminiscent of the light, atmosphere, and landforms of the Arctic.

I began work on *Clouds* immediately after the death of my father, in early 1991. By March of that year I had completed a forty-minute fragment for large orchestra. The press of other commitments forced me to set this aside. Over the next five and a half years I returned to *Clouds* as time allowed, following as it evolved through various forms and instrumentations. I worked on it throughout 1994 during a fellowship from the Foundation for Contemporary Performance Arts, finally completing it in late 1995.

In composing *Clouds* I was determined to sustain an uncompromising faith in the musical materials, surrendering self-expression for trust in the instruments and the essential richness inherent within their sounds. In retrospect, I believe the only significant compromises in this music resulted from the limitations of my own concentration and imagination.

New Songs

As a composer I've dedicated my life to the creation of new music. But when I first began to learn the music of Alaska's Native peoples my favorite songs were the old songs, songs which often celebrated traditional subsistence activities—hunting, fishing, traveling by kayak. At festivals, when a dance group would perform a newer song that celebrated riding on a snow machine or playing basketball, and maybe incorporated elements from Western music, I'd sit through it impatiently waiting for the next traditional song.

Then one evening at the Festival of Native Arts, during a performance by an especially strong Yup'ik dance group, I realized the hypocrisy of my attitude. It suddenly dawned on me that these songs about snow machines and basketball are every bit as "authentic" as the old songs about seal hunting, steam baths, or berry picking. Just like new music in Western traditions, these new indigenous songs are cause for celebration. The fact that Native people are composing songs about their lives today is proof positive that their cultures are alive and well. This is a cause for celebration and a great hope for the future.

Now whenever I hear a new song from any culture, I listen carefully.

Roots and Influences (2000–2001)

Like many composers of my generation, I grew up playing rock 'n' roll. As a kid I took piano lessons, sang in choirs, and played trumpet in school bands and orchestras. But it was playing drums and singing in a series of garage bands that really got me excited about music. My first bands covered tunes by the Beatles, the Kinks, the Rolling Stones, and other big groups of the day.

As time went on we got tired of just rehashing other people's songs and started writing a few of our own. The deeper we got into songwriting the broader and more adventurous our listening became. Yes, Jimi Hendrix. But also John Coltrane, Soft Machine, Captain Beefheart, Ornette Coleman, Frank Zappa. On the back of his early records, Zappa used to print this defiant little epigram: " 'The present-day composer refuses to die!' — Edgard Varèse." My buddies and I would read that, scratch our heads, and wonder: "Hmmm. Just who is this VaREEsee guy?" Then one day in the local record shop (this must have been about 1967), my friend Richard Einhorn discovered one of the first Varèse LPs. We quickly wore out the grooves.

From Zappa to Varèse, it didn't take long for us to discover Cage, Stockhausen, Xenakis, Partch, Oliveros, Reich, Nancarrow. and a whole new world of music. One of the epiphanies of my life came when I acquired a Columbia Masterworks LP titled "Morton Feldman: The Early Years." All I really knew about Feldman was that he was a pal of John Cage. But when I heard the *Piece for Four Pianos*, I thought I'd died and gone to heaven. This music took me to a place that Pink Floyd just couldn't go. It was right about then that I decided I had to be a composer.

A major element in my early musical education was listening

These thoughts are drawn from correspondence with the musicologist Sabine Feisst.

to recordings. I devoured everything I could get my ears on. I also learned a lot by reading books and studying scores. I had a couple of friends—the other members of my last rock-based trio—who were also discovering new music at the same time. Together we did a lot of improvising, trying out things we'd heard in the music of Cage, Stockhausen, and others. We also wrote pieces for ourselves. Some of these were conventionally notated. Others used graphic notation or word instructions.

I never graduated from high school. But in 1970–71 (which would have been my senior year) I studied music at Mercer University. I took piano and voice lessons, theory and ear training, sang in the choir, and played percussion in the pit orchestra for musicals. At the same time I studied composition privately with Fred Coulter. Fred taught me twelve-tone and other serial techniques, and gave me very important early confirmation that I could be a composer. This all happened when I was seventeen and eighteen. It was an explosive time of discovery for me. In many respects it set the direction of my entire creative life.

I submitted a portfolio of my compositions to Cal Arts. Sadly, I no longer have those scores or tapes. (I destroyed them in a post-adolescent moment of redefining myself.) But I remember a piece for violin and tape, an open-form piece for unspecified instruments, a short piece for prepared piano, and several pieces for two pianos.

By the time I arrived at Cal Arts, I had read Cage's *Silence* and Harry Partch's *Genesis of a Music*. (I first read Henry Cowell's *New Musical Resources* in the summer of 1972, after my first year at Cal Arts. I found it in a record and bookshop in Washington, D.C., where I worked that summer.) I was at Cal Arts for two years, and it was absolutely the right time and place for me. My alternative choice was Columbia. But I can't imagine what would have become of me musically had I not chosen Cal Arts. The school was brand new. The facilities were fantastic and the faculty was even more exciting. James Tenney, Leonard Stein, Mel Powell,

Harold Budd, Charlemagne Palestine, Ingram Marshall, and Morton Subotnick were all there. My fellow students included Peter Garland, David Mahler, William Winant, and Carl Stone. I felt lost in Los Angeles, but the place made an environmentalist out of me and set me off in search of home, which eventually led me to Alaska.

Tenney was the perfect teacher for me. He allowed me to make my own mistakes and my own discoveries. And he had an uncanny knack for asking just the right question at just the right moment. I think my greatest debt to him has to do with the essential unity of sound and form. I've long been fascinated with Tenney's ideas about form as an object of perception. I'm especially taken with his concept of "ergodic" form—an entire piece conceived and perceived as a single sound. In my own music I try to combine rigorous formalism with an equally intense sensuality (the legacy of Feldman), and an integration of pitch and rhythm (the theoretical legacy of Cowell). Tenney also gave me a strong sense of connecting with the experimentalist tradition from Charles Ives to Lou Harrison to Pauline Oliveros. (Recently the practitioners of this tradition have been popularized as the "American Mavericks." But in 1971 very few people recognized the importance of these composers.) Most of all Tenney taught by example. The strength of his music and his fierce commitment to both intellectual rigor and sounding acoustical truth set the highest possible standards for me.

Along with Cowell's and Partch's books, Tenney's writings about harmony and form, and Kyle Gann's writings about the music of Nancarrow and La Monte Young have been very important to me. I have the greatest respect for Tenney, Young, Gann, Larry Polansky, Alvin Lucier, and other composers who are also brilliant theoreticians. Tenney has often said that his primary motivation for composing is curiosity. Many of his pieces seem to originate with a question: "What would it sound like if . . ." A similar spirit of inquiry seems to drive Lucier's work. But despite strong theoretical foundations, the real power of the music of these composers is its singularity of the sound.

Chaos theory, quantum physics, and more recently color theory have all absorbed my interest. At a certain point, though, I find myself inspired less by technical details and more by the metaphor, the poetics of theory. I love acoustics and psychoacoustics. I sometimes read books on these subjects just to renew my sense of wonder about the nature of sound. To me it's a lot like reading poetry.

Ultimately, theory is a means to an end. The end is the sounding music. The real substance and value of theory lie in its resonance with nature, its power to expand and deepen our perceptions of the world. And in the world of music, everything eventually comes back to the sound.

Fixing stylistic labels to music is tricky. These days when people ask me what kind of music I compose, I usually tell them: "My music." Then I go on to describe the sound of the music, the influences, metaphors, and the media of my work.

My music has sometimes been called "minimalist" or "post-minimalist." To most people the term minimalism calls to mind short rhythmic cells, slow-moving, consonant harmonies, and audible compositional processes. However, I rarely use literal repetition in my music. Something is always changing, even when the surface sounds more or less the same.

Much of my music does embrace consonance and modal harmony. But a work like *Clouds of Forgetting, Clouds of Unknowing* is relentlessly chromatic and dissonant. *Strange and Sacred Noise* celebrates unmitigated noise, and the tuning world of *Earth and the Great Weather* is derived directly from the harmonic series.

Though I aspire to rigorous form and construction in my music, I no longer want my compositional processes to be immediately audible. Audible processes seem to me to constitute a kind of linear narrative that I want to leave behind. I want the music to feel inevitable as it unfolds. But instead of the arc of a story, I want the music to have the more objective presence of a place.

Minimalism was an important influence in my earlier days. It's definitely one of the seeds from which my music grew. But I don't think the minimalist or post-minimalist label really fits the music. I've always felt more directly connected with the American experimentalist tradition from Ives and Cowell to Partch, Nancarrow, Cage, Feldman, Harrison, Oliveros, and Tenney. These are my deepest musical roots.

In his writings Kyle Gann has discussed my music along with the work of Mikel Rouse, Lois Vierk, Michael Gordon, Larry Polansky, and others as part of a movement he calls "totalism." Although I admire the work of these composers, I was initially skeptical about having my music included under this rubric. As Gann puts it, totalism is a desire "to have your cake and eat it, too" —to write music that has the rhythmic energy of rock and the intellectual substance of "classical" music. Until recently I've understood this to imply rhythmic complexity in relation to a regular pulse, and a broad range of musical influences. Lately, however, it's struck me that a deeper implication of the term may be the ideal of integrating harmony and rhythm into a unified field grounded in the harmonic series—a "totality" of pitch and time. This idea, of course, dates back to Cowell. And I'm a lot more comfortable with this take on totalism.

My concept of "sonic geography" sometimes seems to link me with an international community of "soundscape" artists and the acoustic ecology movement. I feel a certain philosophical affinity with R. Murray Schafer, Annea Lockwood, Hildegard Westerkamp, David Dunn, and other artists whose work is grounded in soundscape. Yet I don't feel my work is part of that movement. I've only utilized recordings of environmental sounds in a single work (*Earth and the Great Weather*). And I'm more interested in evoking the *feeling* of nature than the sound of nature.

The musicologist Mitchell Morris (in his essay "Ecotopian Sounds: Strong Environmentalism and The Music of John Luther Adams") refers to me as a "Green composer." I don't object to this. After all, I have been active in the Green Party in Alaska. But the context of my work goes beyond environmental activism and Green politics to a larger sense of place and culture. So I interpret Morris's use of the term "Green" in relation to my music as cultural and philosophical rather than narrowly political.

I've never intended my works as pure environmental statements. And although everything I do is in some way influenced by the North, I balk at being categorized as a "regionalist." My aspiration is that the music extends beyond the place from which it's born.

The Same Language

The text of *Earth and the Great Weather* is a series of *Arctic Litanies*, composed from the names of places, directions, seasons, plants, and birds. Writing these found poems was a continuing revelation of the deep connections between Alaska Native languages and the places from which they come.

I was working on *River with No Willows*, the litany of plants. I'd compiled long lists of plant names in English, Latin, and Gwich'in. But I had very few in Iñupiaq.

I went to James Nageak.

"James. I'm working on the plants, and I can't find many Iñupiaq names. Can you recommend a good source?"

"Not really," he said.

"Well, let me show you what I have."

We read through my short list.

"Yeah. That's pretty much it," said James.

"Come on," I said. "You guys have lived in the Arctic since time immemorial. There are all kinds of plants up there."

James grinned at me and quipped: "We don't eat a lot of salad."

A couple of weeks later, the tables were turned.

We were rehearsing *One That Stays All Winter*, the litany of birds. In the middle of the piece Lincoln Tritt intoned an especially resonant name in his Gwich'in dialect: ". . . Aahaalak . . ."

A few seconds later, James echoed: "Aaqhaaliq."

Everybody stopped.

James looked at Lincoln. "You said 'Aaqhaaliq.'"

Lincoln looked at James. "You said 'Aahaalak.'"

As it turns out, the name for the oldsquaw duck is the same in both Iñupiaq and Gwich'in.

The call of the oldsqaw is onomatopoetic. The bird sings its own name.

To this day James and Lincoln always greet one another with a hearty call: "A-haa-lik!"

Beyond Expression (2001)

In the nineteenthth century, Western music was swept away by the cult of the composer—the solitary hero whose trials and triumphs provided the plot for extended musical narratives and dramas. But in the larger context of history Romanticism was an anomaly. It seems to me that much Western music before and since contemplates something more transpersonal, some deeper mysteries inherent in the sounds of voices, instruments, and time.

A central part of the Romantic ethos was the mystique of the masterwork. By nineteenth-century standards new music doesn't often measure up. But those standards no longer apply—at least not in the same way.

A few years ago a reviewer of one of my works took me to task for aspiring to create a masterpiece. Guilty as charged. Like the late Morton Feldman, I still believe in the solitary masterpiece. But in our time (as in the centuries before the Romantic era) the master is not the composer. It's the music.

Willem de Kooning had the right idea about history when he said: "I'm not influenced by the past. I influence it." (The irony, of course, is that in some respects he was the most old-fashioned artist of his time.) Jackson Pollock made a related quip. When asked why he didn't work from nature, Pollock fired back: "I *am* nature."

True enough. The natural world is the most fundamental source of human intelligence, creativity, and culture. We don't truly create anything except answers to creation. And we're an inseparable part of nature. But in recent times we've forgotten this.

These thoughts first appeared in the September 2001 issue of *NewMusicBox*

In the nineteenth century European composers celebrated Romantic individualism and the rise of the middle class in industrial society. At the same time the West lost touch with our intimate connections to the Earth. And over the past two centuries the land and water, the wild animals, and the indigenous peoples of the world have paid a terrible price. The dream of unlimited material prosperity has brought us overpopulation, over consumption, rampant pollution, global climate change, numerous wars, and a world in which much of the wealth is controlled by a handful of gigantic corporations.

The challenge for artists today is to move beyond self-expression and beyond anthropocentric views of history, to re-imagine and re-create our relationships with this planet and all those (human and other-than-human) with whom we share it. I believe that music, art, and literature in the twenty-first century must embody this change. If artists lead, society will eventually follow. And our own survival may literally depend on it: As we treat the world, so we treat ourselves.

Art can be and in some ways must be intensely personal. But personal statements alone are not enough. Art has the power to take us beyond ourselves, to remind us of the larger, deeper miracles of the world. We need to remember these miracles in everything we do.

In the Ears of the Listener

I went into a busy music store in New York City to buy a pair of loudspeakers for my studio. The salesman suggested I compare the different makes and models by listening to something I knew well.

"Do you have any of your own work with you?" he asked.

As it turned out, I did.

As rock guitarists attacked power chords in the next room, I listened to a passage from *Dream in White on White*, with harp, string quartet, and string orchestra playing in non-tempered tuning and several simultaneous tempos. The salesman went about his business, catching up on paperwork behind the counter.

Next, to test low frequency response at high dynamic levels, I played a section of thundering glaciers and drums from *Earth and the Great Weather*. The salesman looked up briefly, then returned to what he was doing.

Finally I cued a radically different selection from *Earth*. Soft string harmonics trilled with the delicate tinkling of glacial ice and voices whispering in four languages—all on the threshold of audibility.

The salesman looked up again, cocked his head to one side, and listened intently for a moment with a gently quizzical expression on his face. He walked over, stood beside me, and said, quite earnestly:

"Yes. But do you have anything with *music*?"

Strange and Sacred Noise (1998)

Nothing essential happens in the absence of noise . . .
in most cultures, the theme of noise lies at the origin of the
religious idea . . .

Music, then, constitutes communication with this primordial,
threatening noise — prayer.
—Jacques Attali

My music is haunted by place, and by an ideal of *sonic geography* — place as music, and music as place. More recently I've begun to explore new aspects of the relationships between music and place, in a convergence of sonic geography with sonic *geometry*.

We often think of music as a kind of language, which of course it can be. But rather than a music of discourse, mine is a music of the sounding image. My concern is not with musical "ideas" and the rhetoric of composition, but with the singular sonority — that sound which stands for nothing other than itself, filling time and space with the vivid, physical *presence* of a place.

For many years now I've listened carefully to the sounds of the natural world and attempted to translate what I've heard there into my own music. Initially I was attracted to the songs of birds and other more "poetic" dimensions of the soundscape. But gradually I've been drawn to the "noisier" sounds of nature — ocean waves and waterfalls, storm winds and thunder, glaciers crashing into the sea — those elemental voices which resonate so profoundly in the human mind and spirit.

Some time ago, during a period of personal crisis, I camped

This essay first appeared in the *Yearbook of Soundscape Studies*.

alone in early spring on the banks of the Yukon River, listening to the sounds of the great river breaking free from the frozen stillness of winter. The glassy tones of candle ice swirling in a whirlpool, the intricate arpeggios of melt water dripping, and the ominous rumbling and grinding of icebergs struck resonances deep within me. Immersed in these sounds and in the arresting presence of that elemental violence, my personal concerns began to seem small and inconsequential.

The awesome and indifferent forces of nature are stark reminders of the insignificance of our personal dramas and passions. They offer us undeniable reassurance that whatever we may inflict upon ourselves and on one another, there are processes at work in the world far larger, older, and more complex than we can understand.

Standing on the bank of a great river at breakup or near a tidewater glacier as a massive wall of ice explodes into the sea, we are confronted with the overwhelming violence of nature—a violence at once terrifying and comforting, transpersonal and purifying.

The subject matter of creation is chaos.
—Barnett Newman

My growing fascination with the violence of nature led me to a rudimentary study of chaos theory, fractal geometry, and the science of complexity—recent attempts by Western science to describe the rich patterns of the world. As I contemplated the strange beauty of fractal forms and processes, my composer's curiosity was aroused. Quite naturally I wondered: How might these intriguing phenomena *sound*?

My first explorations of this question came in *Strange and Sacred Noise*—an extended cycle of pieces for percussion quartet, combining my long-standing passion for sounds and images from the natural world with a newly found fascination for the mathematics of dynamic systems. In this music I attempted to translate a few of the reiterated, self-similar forms of simple fractals into sound and time, in search of their audible equivalents.

Chaos theory arrives at the most complex of ends from the simplest of means. In painting Mark Rothko spoke of his similar aspiration to "the simple expression of the complex thought." In that spirit, I began my investigation of fractals as music with the simplest of forms: the so-called "classical" fractals created by linear, iterative processes. Compared with the mind-boggling complexities of the more familiar non-linear fractals, these forms are relatively simple. Still, they offer intriguing enigmas and rich metaphors.

I wanted to get a "hands-on" feel for the behavior of these forms and processes, so rather than rely on a computer for composition or generation of the sounds, I composed scores in conventional notation to be played by human performers on acoustical instruments. I wanted to savor the learning, weighing the full resonance of the fundamental principles inherent in these simplest fractals before moving into more complex territory.

Form is idealized space. Sound is audible time. Form defines a context. Sound embodies the presence of the moment.

As in much of my work the musical forms of *Strange and Sacred Noise* are large, simple, and symmetrical. Overall symmetry helps me break free of the conventions of composition by relationship.

Symmetry is predictable: One equals one. It neutralizes questions about where the music is "going" or what will happen next. If the next sound is inevitable, then it's free to stand only for itself. Without the expectations of narrative development or "the element of surprise," both the composer and listener are free simply to listen to the music.

Composing within audible forms, as James Tenney once succinctly put it, "The composer isn't privy to anything." Although I feel free to break the symmetry at any time, I try to do so primarily in response to the physical characteristics of the instruments or the practical realities of performance and notation, rather than

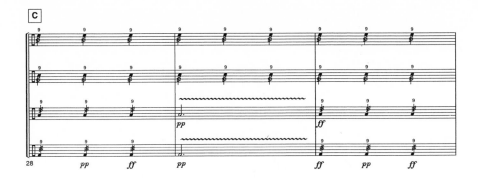

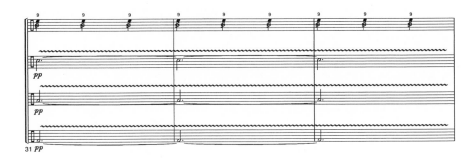

From Strange and Sacred Noise

133

from my own ideas of what should happen next. Morton Feldman did this with an exquisite touch. He called his forms "crippled symmetry" (in fact, that's the title of one of his later works). I think this is also something of what Barnett Newman meant when he spoke of "busting the geometry" in his paintings.

I want my music to have both formal rigor and visceral impact. Through the discipline of an overall formal symmetry, I hope to move beyond self-expression and the limits of my own imagination to a deeper awareness of the sound itself. Occasionally I feel compelled to break the form in order to transcend it. But as both listener and composer I'm most deeply moved when the music has little or nothing to do with personal expression.

In *Strange and Sacred Noise* my interest was not in sending messages, but in receiving them. This is not music as communication, but music as communion. At times during the seven years in which I worked on this cycle, I wondered whether this was music at all. Its dynamics range from the threshold of audibility to the threshold of pain. It embraces unsettling timbres and virtually the entire audible spectrum of sound. Its dense, nearly static fields of sound seem to invite boredom. But my touchstone throughout was a deepening faith in the power of noise as a vehicle of transformation and revelation.

Ultimately, I've come to regard the six sections of *Strange and Sacred Noise* not so much as musical compositions or pieces, but as *places*—places for listening, places in which to experience the elemental mystery of noise. Much of this music is loud. It buzzes the eardrums, rattles the ribcage, and immerses the listener in an overwhelming physical presence of sound. Some of that presence is not actually written on the page. It arises spontaneously in the air, through the dynamic interplay of complex, high-energy sounds (thundering drums, roaring tam-tams, hammered bells, wailing sirens), the acoustics of the performance space, and the psychoacoustics of our own hearing.

If *Strange and Sacred Noise* asks unusual attentiveness of the lis-

From *Strange and Sacred Noise*

135

tener, it places extraordinary demands on the performers—both musically and physically. It demands unflinching intensity of concentration, sustained, vigorous athleticism, and at times the quiet intensity and slow equipoise of Yoga or Tai Chi. Although a performance of this music is visually and sonically dramatic, this is not so much theater as it is ritual—a ceremony in search of a shared experience of transcendence.

The strange power of noise can open doorways to the ecstatic. Musical traditions throughout the world have explored this power for centuries. My own most powerful experience of this has been through the all-night drumming, chant, and dance ceremonies of the Iñupiat and Yup'ik peoples—ceremonies that alter the consciousness of listeners and participants, through the rapid and insistent reiteration of loud, acoustically-complex sounds.

Beyond the usual expressive associations of "musical" sounds, noise touches and moves us in profound ways. Through its sheer physicality, noise commands our attention and breaks down the barriers we construct between our selves and our awareness. Immersed in the enveloping presence of elemental noise in the fullness of the present moment, we just may begin to hear, with the whole of the self, something of the inaudible totality of sound.

The Light That Fills the World (2000)

My fears,
those small ones
that I thought so big,
for all the vital things
I had to get and to reach.

When, in fine weather,
I drifted out too far in my kayak
And thought myself in danger.

And yet there is only
one great thing,
the only thing:

To live to see in huts and on journeys
the great day that dawns,
and the light that fills the world.
—Inuit song

For much of the year, the world in which I live is a vast, white canvas.

Last winter, reading the art critic John Gage's essay *Color as Subject*, I was struck by the equivalence between the view out my window and Mark Rothko's use of white in his paintings. The exquisite colors on the snow and those in Rothko's translucent fields suggested to me broad washes of harmony and timbre, floating in what Morton Feldman called "time undisturbed."

The ideal of the sublime landscape has long been a fundamental metaphor for my work. But the resonances of my recent musical landscapes are more introverted, a little less obviously connected with the external world. If in the past the melodic elements of the music have somehow spoken of my own subjective presence in the landscape, in the newer music there are no lines left—only slowly changing light on a timeless white field. All the edges are blurred. All the sounds meld into one unbroken aural horizon. Harmony and color become fused with space and time.

These seemingly static fields of sound embrace constant change. But rather than moving on a journey through a musical landscape, the experience of listening is more like sitting in the same place while the wind and weather, the light and shadows slowly change. The longer we stay in one place, the more we notice change.

The Light That Fills the World was written in late winter and early spring, when after the long darkness of winter the world is still white and filled with new light. If the unrelenting texture of this music embodies stasis, I hope its prevalent tone evokes the ecstatic. The title of the piece is borrowed from an Inuit song that sings of the close relationship between beauty and terror, risk and revelation.

Practicing What She Preaches

For much of his life John Cage had no interest in harmony. But in his later years he said he found a new appreciation and understanding of harmony, through the music of James Tenney and Pauline Oliveros.

Pauline has taken as her life work a seemingly simple but very demanding discipline: Always listen.

Once I participated in a symposium with Pauline. A discussion arose about some trivial point of aesthetics. At first I found the exchange mildly amusing. To my left Pauline sat perfectly still, hands folded in her lap, eyes closed.

Gradually the discussion escalated into a debate. I grew bored. Pauline sat motionless. As the tone of the rhetoric became more and more contentious, I became more and more frustrated. But the more heated the words, the more beatific Pauline's countenance became.

When the session was finally over, I turned to Pauline and said: "That was torture! How on earth could you sit there like a bodhisattva in the midst of all that nonsense?"

With a knowing smile and a gentle chuckle, Pauline replied: "Oh, I was listening to the reverberations and resonance frequencies of the room, and the beautiful way that sounds travel in this space . . . I wasn't listening to the *words!*"

In the White Silence (1998)

White is not the absence of color. It is the fullness of light.

Silence is not the absence of sound. It is the presence of stillness.

As the Inuit have known for centuries, and as painters from Kasimir Malevich to Robert Ryman have shown us more recently, whiteness embraces many hues, textures, and nuances.

As John Cage reminded us, silence does not literally exist. Still, in a world going deaf with human noise, silence endures as a deep and resonant metaphor.

In his *Poetics of Music* Stravinsky speaks of music as a form of philosophical speculation. But music can also be a form of contemplation: the sensual reaching for the spiritual.

I aspire to music that is both rigorous in thought and sensuous in sound.

I've long been obsessed with the notion of music as place and place as music. The treeless, windswept expanses of the Arctic are enduring creative touchstones for my work, and *In the White Silence* is an attempt to evoke an enveloping musical presence equivalent to that of a vast tundra landscape.

But I want to go beyond landscape painting with tones, beyond language, metaphor, and the extra-musical image. I want to leave the composition, the "piece" of music, for the *wholeness* of music.

I no longer want to be outside the music, listening to it as an object apart. I want to *inhabit* the music, to be fully present and listening in that immeasurable space that Malevich called "a desert of pure feeling."

From In the White Silence

River Music

Gordon Wright is one of my closest friends. But our musical interests don't always coincide. Gordon is the last Romantic. During his long career he's conducted much of the nineteenth-century symphonic repertoire and has made a name for himself as an advocate of works by forgotten Romantics. On the other hand, it would be an understatement to say that I've never been much interested in Romantic music.

Beyond our differing musical inclinations, Gordon and I share a deep love for wilderness. Over the years we've taken a number of memorable trips together. Late one August we decided to float a stretch of the upper Tanana River, near the Canadian border. As we sped down the Alaska Highway in his old Toyota wagon, Gordon put on a recording of Bruckner's Symphony no. 8. I was transfixed. The soaring lines and harmonic sweep of the music resonated perfectly with the expanse of mountains and forests all around us. The Adagio in particular went right to my soul. When the music stopped, I heaved a sigh and said to Gordon: "This may be where our musical worlds meet."

As we floated down the river over the next several days, the reverberations continued. At the end of our trip I found myself shuttling Gordon's car from the take-out spot back to the put-in. I drove with Bruckner playing at top volume.

Ever since that trip down the Tanana I've been a confirmed Brucknerphile. From Bruckner, I've gone on to approach Wagner. I haven't yet warmed up to Mahler. I recognize that Mahler is a greater composer than Bruckner. Still I love Bruckner because his music is about something larger, something far beyond the composer.

Bruckner's faith was in the church. My faith is in the earth. But like Bruckner, I aspire to music as a vehicle of transcendence. Now whenever I think of that stretch of the Tanana, I hear the Adagio of the Bruckner Eighth in my mind. And whenever I hear Bruckner, I think of the river.

Credo (2002)

I have faith. But it has no name.

My faith is grounded in the earth, in the relationships between all beings and all things, and in the practice of music as a spiritual discipline.

These thoughts first emerged from a pre-concert discussion in response to the question: "What is your faith?" They evolved further in correspondence with the writer and translator Alain Sainte-Marie, who was writing about the influence of the medieval mystical text The Cloud of Unknowing on contemporary artists.

Through my experiences in the wilderness and from the wisdom of my friends and neighbors the Iñupiat, Athabascan, and Yup'ik peoples of Alaska, I've come to recognize all the plants and animals, and the land itself, as my relatives, my family. This awareness of "the spirit in all things" has become central to my own faith.

Over the years also I've come to understand my life's work in music as the practice of my faith. I aspire to composition, performance, and listening to music as forms of contemplation.

Although I've never been a regular practitioner of any established spiritual tradition, from time to time I've felt resonance with certain traditions. Zen Buddhism was the first to engage me. I came to it as a young man, through the music and writings of John Cage. Through Zen I discovered Thomas Merton. My parents were Episcopal and I was confirmed in that church. But Merton's brand of Christianity was the first to resonate with me. His writings have meant a lot to me, especially *New Seeds of Contemplation*. I've also been moved by *The Way of a Pilgrim*. And I still turn to a Gnostic Book of Hours from time to time.

After the death of my father I discovered *The Cloud of Unknowing*. I found comfort and inspiration in its pages as I worked on my composition *Clouds of Forgetting, Clouds of Unknowing*, which is dedicated to the memory of my father.

Like most of the world's ancient religions, Christianity feels to me like a complete and beautiful ecosystem. Yet it seems as different from my spiritual world as the tropical rainforest is from the boreal forest of my home. I'm grateful for the rainforest and I pray for its health, its wholeness, its continuation. But the boreal forest is where I live, and Alaska Native traditions feel much closer to my heart and home. Still, I don't belong to these cultures and I can't claim their traditions as my own. So ultimately music and the natural world seem to be as close to religion as I get.

In the Sweet Bye and Bye (2000)

A few days ago, shortly after takeoff, Alaska Airlines Flight 261 crashed into the ocean north of Los Angeles. There were no survivors. When we heard the news, my wife Cindy said to me: "We probably knew someone on that plane." She was right.

Morris Thompson, his wife Thelma, and their daughter Sheryl were on Flight 261. Morris was one of the most prominent political leaders in the state. In essence he was the governor of Athabascan Alaska. We didn't always agree with his politics, but we always admired and respected Morrie for his gentle manner, his generous spirit, and his unshakeable dedication to his people. Thelma was the sister of my Athabascan "brother," Clyde Mayo. Thelma was the second sister Clyde has lost in a year.

This week Cindy and I have spent as much time as we could with Clyde and his wife Kathy. All week long there's been a vigil at the tribal center. People have come from all over Alaska to remember, to share songs and stories, and to comfort the family. At Kathy's and Clyde's house, Cindy has helped the women bake, while I've helped the men pick up and deliver salmon, halibut, moose, caribou, and other wild foods—gifts flown in from the southeastern rainforest to the Arctic coast—to be prepared for the memorial potlatch. In the midst of tragedy the family exhibits remarkable strength and dignity. Native people are all too familiar with this kind of grief.

The memorial for the Thompsons is held in the largest room in town: the hockey rink. Hundreds of people—Native and non-Native, people from all viewpoints and all stations in life—are here to pay their respects and to celebrate the lives of Morrie, Thelma, and Sheryl.

The ceremony is a uniquely Alaskan amalgam of Native and Western, religious and secular elements. An Episcopal priest leads the proceedings, but the principal speakers are family members, community leaders, and Native elders. Emotion is high and there are many tearful eyes.

Throughout the service there is singing. All of us join in singing songs and hymns that were favorites of Morrie and Thelma. Toward the end, we sing "In the Sweet Bye and Bye." Cindy and I hold hands, trying to hold back the tears.

The song ends and the priest moves toward the podium. But before he can speak, from far up in the grandstands an old woman with a high, frail voice resumes singing the refrain of the song, in the Koyukon dialect. Other women around her join in. My skin turns to goose flesh.

As they reach the final cadence and stop singing, another group of women on the other side of the cavernous space takes up the tune, this time in Gwich'in. Tears flow down my face. The sense of loss and grief in this moment are beyond words. But equally palpable is the feeling of surrender and transcendence.

After the memorial is the potlatch, the traditional Native ceremony of feasting, oration, and celebration. The meal consists of traditional subsistence foods—moose, caribou, maktak, and fish of all kinds. Several hundred of us are served by the extended family and people from Morrie's home village of Tanana. Once seated at a potlatch, you remain seated to the end. Whatever food is offered, you accept with gratitude. These are matters of courtesy and respect.

As a child, I was confirmed in the Episcopal church. But potlatch is a more meaningful to me than the Eucharist ever was. Here in this hockey rink, surrounded by community, we celebrate the circle of life and death in a communion that joins people and animals with the land and the waters that we share.

"... the lines disappear completely ..." (2001)

Number 5, 1950 was Mark Rothko's last painting before the breakthrough into his mature format. In it the luminous color fields of a classic Rothko are inscribed across the middle with three delicate lines.

Describing this painting and its pivotal position in Rothko's work, Brian O'Doherty observes: "After this, the lines disappear completely."

In 1988, after the première of *The Far Country of Sleep*, my friend Leif Thompson made a prophetic observation: "I especially like that middle section," he said to me. "You know, the part where nothing happens. That's what you really want to do, isn't it?"

Leif was right. And a decade later, in *The Immeasurable Space of Tones* and *The Light That Fills the World*, I finally took that leap.

But if these works constitute a breakthrough in my music, it was a long time coming. From the earliest works in my catalog I now hear an inexorable evolution to this new sound world. Over the course of twenty-five years, line and figuration gradually disappear. What began as background has finally advanced into the foreground to become a musical world composed entirely of floating fields of color.

It seems almost impossible to consider musical color without considering timbre, which we sometimes call "tone color." But in *The Light, Immeasurable Space* and subsequent works I've tried to create color not so much through timbre as through harmony. Specific instrumental timbres are less important than the harmonic voicing and the registers of the tones. The density of tones and the tempo relationships between the different layers of the music give shape to the colors. In a sense the music is independent of timbre, lending itself to different combinations of instruments without losing its fundamental coloration.

As this new sound-world has emerged I've changed media, moving from the orchestra to smaller mixed ensembles of electronic and acoustical instruments. I still think in orchestral terms. But scale is not a matter of size. It is perceived dimension. And these smaller ensembles allow me to create expansive orchestral textures in a more practical and available medium. The medium is different but the sense of space, the scale of the music, is the same.

Searching for what Kandinsky called "those inner sounds that are the life of the colors," I begin by combining intervals into chords and modes, building my palette of harmonic hues. Mixing the chromatic density of the harmonies (pentatonic, diatonic, octatonic, chromatic) creates the saturation of the colors. And register, the octave placement of tones, is my equivalent of brightness, with the highest registers the brightest and the lowest registers the darkest.

Composition can wait. The colors come first. And even when composition begins, I try to keep the composer's touch as light as possible, letting the forms and textures grow out of the colors, searching for what Kirk Varnedoe calls in Pollock's poured paintings "an orchestration of untouched material."

Not long ago I revisited Mondrian. Looking at photographs of his sketches I was struck by their similarity to Rothko's rectangles. Compositionally Mondrian's sketches resemble even more Richard Diebenkorn's Ocean Park paintings. Whether filled with color (as in Rothko and Diebenkorn) or described only by black lines on empty white fields (as in Mondrian's sketches), the dynamic balances of the forms are strikingly similar.

Rothko is widely regarded as a colorist, but he thought of himself as a formalist. It's not only the colors. It's the shapes, the proportions, and the edges of his forms that give his colors their extraordinary power. Even when the subject is color, the forms of the colors describe lines.

In music, line, form, and color are equally inseparable. The moment one chord changes to another we hear the beginning of a line. And the moment a single tone moves we begin to hear harmony. It might seem that the only harmony we wouldn't hear melodically would be a harmony that never changes. But in his *Dream House* installations, La Monte Young has revealed rich melodic worlds within unchanging harmonic clouds. We might imagine that the only melody we wouldn't hear harmonically would be a melody on one note. But Giacinto Scelsi discovered expansive harmonic richness within a solitary tone.

At first I imagined my "color" works as a kind of monophonic or monolithic music—an entire piece as one rich and complex sound. Gradually I came to hear them as homophonic textures—like extraordinarily slow chorales unfolding over the course of an entire piece. Now, after composing several works in this world that I had thought was completely free of lines, I've come to hear it as a sort of polyphony of harmonic clouds.

So maybe the lines never disappear completely. Maybe Christian Wolff was right when he quipped: "No matter what we do, sooner or later it all sounds melodic."

Remembering Lou (2003)

The great redwood has fallen.
Light streams into the forest.
The sound will reverberate
for generations to come.

The passing of Lou Harrison marks the end of an era in American music that began with Charles Ives and continued on through Henry Cowell, Ruth Crawford Seeger, Harry Partch, Conlon Nancarrow, and John Cage.

The expressive range, diversity of media, prolific quantity, and consistent quality of Lou's music are perhaps unequalled among recent composers. From heroically dissonant orchestral counterpoint to explosive percussive rhythms to ravishing, timeless music for gamelan, his body of work embraces most of the important currents in the music of our time.

Lou always fearlessly pursued his own way. While still a young man, he left the competitive careerism of New York City to make his home on the California coast. There, surrounded by the beauties of nature and the richness of Pacific cultures, he created his own uniquely personal world, grounded in his credo: "Cherish. Conserve. Consider. Create."

As a teacher Lou introduced many young Western musicians to the music of other cultures, or as he called it, "the whole, wide, wonderful world of music." His diminutive *Music Primer* remains a wellspring of creative wisdom about the life and the craft of a composer.

Through his wide-ranging friendships, Lou was a central figure, connecting five generations of musical independents. His spirit lives on in his music and through the immeasurable gifts he gave to so many younger musicians. I feel blessed to have been among them.

Thirty years ago, as an aspiring young composer, I won second place in a composition contest. I was especially thrilled since one of the judges was Lou Harrison, whose music I very much admired. Emboldened, I made the pilgrimage to San Jose State University, where Lou was teaching at the time. I was delighted to find the man himself to be every bit as scintillating and engaging as his music.

From that day on, Lou was a generous mentor, an attentive friend, and an inspiring model to me, as he has been for many other younger composers. Lou always treated me with respect as a younger colleague. His matter-of-fact embrace of my aspirations removed any shred of doubt in my mind that I would make a life as a composer.

When I first visited Lou and his partner Bill Colvig at their home in Aptos, they picked me up at the bus station in Santa Cruz. Bill was driving and Lou insisted that I ride in the front seat. He wouldn't take no for an answer. From then on, whenever we drove anywhere together this was the seating arrangement. Lou always treated me like visiting royalty.

In my mid-thirties I found myself weighing the risk of quitting my day job to devote myself to composing full-time. My boss offered me the opportunity to continue working half-time. As I often did, I called Lou for his perspective.

As usual, Lou spoke directly to the situation: "There are no half-time jobs, John. Only half-time salaries."

I promptly quit my job and never looked back.

Over the years Lou taught me many lessons about the art of composition and the life of a composer. He also gave me the best conducting lesson I ever had.

In 1988 Lou and Bill came to Alaska for a concert of Lou's

music with the Fairbanks Symphony. On the program was his
Suite for Violin, Piano and Small Orchestra, which I conducted. As a
percussionist I'd always had steady time. And as an occasional
conductor I'd always prided myself on my precision and attention
to detail.

After the dress rehearsal I asked Lou what he thought.

"You remind me of John Cage," he said.

Intrigued and vaguely flattered, I asked: "How so?"

"Well, you're more kinesthetic than John . . ."

I grew more intrigued and more flattered.

"When John used to conduct he wanted to hear every detail of
the music and he tried to show every nuance of the score. So, of
course, the tempo would gradually slow down."

Instantly I recognized that I was doing the very same thing. At
the next night's concert my conducting was leaner, crisper, and
steadier in tempo—a style I've tried to maintain ever since.

This lesson from Lou was not just about conducting. It was
also a lesson about teaching. Lou was fond of recalling that his
teacher Henry Cowell would often begin a sentence by saying "As
you know . . ." and then impart some wonderfully unexpected
pearl of wisdom. In his own teaching Lou employed this technique brilliantly, using the gentle touch of flattery to prepare re-
ceptive minds for the gifts of learning.

For their concert Lou and Bill brought with them the Sunda-
nese *gamelan degung*, Sekar Kembar. As far as we can tell, this
was the first time a gamelan had been heard "live" in Alaska. Bill
played various instruments in the ensemble and he was featured
as a soloist playing the *suling* flute in Lou's tunefully sunny *Main
Bersama-sama* for horn, suling, and gamelan.

This was Lou's one and only visit to Alaska. But it was a home-
coming for Bill. In the late 1930s Bill had left Berkeley to live for
several years on the rough and ready frontier of Alaska and the
Yukon, and he was thrilled to be back in the North again.

After the concert Lou and Bill came out to my cabin for a party. My place was deep in the woods. I had no running water and heated with a wood stove. The temperature in the boreal forest that night was well into the forty-somethings below zero. Accustomed to warmer climes, Lou was good-humored in his forbearance. But Bill was in his element. The colder it got the better he liked it. The aurora borealis dancing in the sky that night was the icing on his cake.

In 1991 I composed *Five Yup'ik Dances*, based on traditional songs of the First People of the Yukon-Kuskokwim delta. These pieces are composed entirely of "white notes," with no sharps or flats. After looking through the score Lou was very enthusiastic, saying: "You've rediscovered those seven tones as something wild, fresh and new." Encouraged by Lou's reaction, I went on to compose *Dream in White on White*—a larger work in Pythagorean diatonic tuning which led eventually to the seventy-five-minute expanse of *In the White Silence*.

Sometime in my mid forties, I began to feel acutely the professional limitations of my life in Alaska. While colleagues elsewhere had blossoming careers, things seemed to be moving very slowly for me. I thought seriously about moving someplace closer to the centers of musical life. I decided to apply for a fellowship and asked Lou if he would write a letter of recommendation for me. Although he was very busy, he cheerfully agreed.

When I received the letter first thing I noticed was the signature, in Lou's incomparable calligraphy. (This was before the development of the lovely "Lou" computer font.) But beyond the elegance of his hand, I was touched by the heart of his message. Among other things Lou observed that by choosing to live in Alaska I had chosen to develop a deep relationship with place and to avoid what he called "the group chattering of the metropolis."

This, he said, had allowed the growth of my work to be "both integrated and in 'real time.'"

Clearly Lou understood the meaning of my life choices better than I did!

I didn't receive the fellowship. But that letter from Lou was an enduring gift. I haven't thought about leaving the North since.

One summer when an orchestral work of mine was performed at the Cabrillo Music Festival, I spent a memorable week with Lou and Bill. After the concert that included my music we had dinner. My piece had been well performed and well received, and I was in an upbeat mood. At the time Lou was enjoying a surge in performances of his orchestral music, and I suggested that this must be gratifying to him.

"It's nice," he said. "But it's not really what we do."

I asked him to elaborate.

"The orchestra is a glorious noise. But the heart and soul of our music lies elsewhere. We're the ones who form our own ensembles, make our own tunings, build our own instruments and create our own musical worlds. We're the 'Do It Yourself' school of American music!"

I was humbled. Here Lou was finally starting to receive from the classical musical establishment some measure of the recognition he deserved, yet he wasn't seduced at all. He always had a singular dedication to the deepest roots of his music and an unwavering sense of who he was.

At a time when gay couples were still largely invisible to the straight world, Lou and Bill openly and tenderly showed their profound love for one another. Their thirty-three years of shared life and devotion are a model and an inspiration for all couples.

As their flowing beards and hair turned white, Lou and Bill grew to resemble one another more and more. When Bill died in 2000, Lou was at his side, holding his hand. "It was a peaceful death," said his soul mate. "He was so beautiful . . . like a beautiful animal returning to Nature."

Like many of their friends, I worried that Lou would soon fol-

The author, Bill Colvig, Lou Harrison. Photo by Dennis Keeley

low Bill. But he continued his life and work with undiminished energy and enthusiasm well into his eighty-sixth year. When he died, he was on his way to a festival of his music.

As Lou once observed: "All good things come to an end. Even the twentieth century!"

Yet Lou Harrison and his joyful, ecumenical life and music seem more vital and pertinent than ever before.

Among Red Mountains (2001)

I've always been intimidated by the piano. As a performer I've never played it very well. And as a composer I've never felt as though I could make the instrument my own.

On a recent trip to New York I heard the première performance of a lovely chamber work by Kyle Gann that embraces multiple tempos without sustaining them all at the same time. On the way home to Alaska I passed through Seattle. In the Seattle airport there's a large painting by Frank Stella. It's one of his protractor works, in which vibrant arcs of color weave in and out of one another in a dizzying counterpoint of imaginary planes. Studying this painting (after hearing Gann's music), it occurred to me that I might be able to do something similar with the piano. Virtually all my recent music has been composed of four, five, or six simultaneous tempo layers. If those ensemble and orchestral pieces are multidimensional sculptures, then *Among Red Mountains* is more like a drawing. In this piece, the challenge I set for myself was to suggest five independent tempo planes, within the limitations of two hands and what the pianist Vicki Ray calls "the Big Black Box."

For three decades I've admired the piano music of Peter Garland. At last I have a piece I hope is worthy of its dedication to him.

The title is the translation of the Gwich'in Athabascan name for a place in the Brooks Range north of Arctic Village.

Among Red Mountains

(for Peter Garland)

John Luther Adams

©Taiga Press 2001

From Among Red Mountains

159

The Heart of the Matter

Allen Otte is one of the most fiercely intelligent musicians I know. He has a rare gift for getting to the heart of whatever musical matter is at hand. And he doesn't mince words.

I had worked with Al and his partners Jim Culley and Rusty Burge (Percussion Group Cincinnati) on previous projects. But our collaboration on *Strange and Sacred Noise* took our friendship— and the music—to the next level.

For quite some time Al and I had talked about my composing a new work specifically for the Percussion Group. I had a concept for an extended cycle inspired by elemental violence and noise. Al liked the idea. But the group is a trio and I was fixated on a quartet. We went back and forth about this for a couple of years— Al trying to convince me that it could be a trio and me trying to convince him that it had to be a quartet.

Finally I sent Al a score and recording of . . . *dust into dust* . . . for four snare drums, along with an outline for the rest of the *Noise* cycle and the draft of an essay about my concept of the work. Not long after, I received a post card written in Al's inimitable calligraphy. It read:

J

    Yes!

        A

We were off and running.

Over the next year or two, as I completed drafts of pieces I'd send them off to Cincinnati, where the group would give them a reading. Sometimes they would send me a tape. And always Al and I would talk over the group's impressions and suggestions.

Noise was strange new territory for all of us and these exchanges were essential to the evolution of the music.

One of the sections in the cycle that gave me particular difficulty was *triadic iteration lattices*. This piece is based on the Sierpinski gasket—a kind of Eiffel Tower fractal. I knew I wanted to sound this form with a web of continuous glissandi, but I couldn't settle on the right instrumentation. After several false starts I sent the group a piece for eight timpani that I hoped might prove to be the sound I was after.

A week or so later, the phone rang. I answered.

"John . . ."

Instantly recognizing the voice and the unique manner of speaking, I replied: "Al . . ."

"It's a piece of shit!"

Instinctively I knew that Al was right. Timpani are made to emphasize the harmonies in the orchestra of Beethoven and Strauss. This new music we were searching for was something far removed from that. Al's pithy critique was exactly the encouragement I needed to venture beyond the boundaries of reason and decorum. The following week I rescored the piece for four sirens. It worked like a charm.

Several months later Percussion Group Cincinnati gave the full première of *Strange and Sacred Noise*. Physically and musically this was an unusually intense and challenging experience for the musicians. After *Noise* Al said that returning to more "normal" music—as a player and a listener—seemed curiously unsatisfying to him.

A couple of weeks later, back home in Alaska, the phone rang. It was Al.

"I just have one question for you," he began.

"OK . . ." I answered.

"*Now* what?!"

I've been working on that question ever since.

The Immeasurable Space
of Tones (2003)

*Even where there is nothing to be seen, nothing to be touched,
nothing to be measured, where bodies do not move from place
to place, there is space . . . the space that tones disclose to us.*
—Victor Zuckerkandl

Morton Feldman's only composition lesson with Varèse
was a brief encounter on a New York street corner. The master
gave the young upstart a single polished pearl of wisdom: "Always
keep in mind how long it takes the sound to travel from here to
there."

That seemingly simple adage contains a world of implications.

The trajectories of sounds articulate the physical, temporal,
and tonal spaces of music. Different instruments speak and resonate differently, and the composer must know how to mix sounds
the way a painter knows how to mix colors. The acoustical spaces
in which we listen profoundly shape our music, and the composer
should be as aware of the listening space as the visual artist is of
the viewing space.

The sound of an instrument travels across space to touch the
drums of the listener's ears. The time this takes is a measure of
the distance between the two. When we measure time we spa-
tialize time. Though sound and time are materials of music, we
often describe them in terms of space. We speak of "high" and
"low" sounds, "lengths" of time, and compositional "forms" and
"structures." We also conceive of musical time in "horizontal"
and "vertical" planes.

Horizontal time is the linear flow of events, one thing following another—from then, into now, into not-yet-now. Horizontal time engages our memory and expectation, framing the past and the future like a window. Our attention moves through horizontal time as through the spaces between foreground, middle ground, and background.

Vertical time is the presence of the moment. Memory and expectation are suspended, reflecting the endless present like a mirror. Our attention is entirely focused on a single, all-encompassing time and place: *here and now.*

In horizontal time we travel from here to there. A tree falls in the forest, but we may not hear it because we've already moved on to the next stop on the journey. In vertical time, with no expectation of moving to another place, we hear not only the sound of the tree falling but the music of the forest listening to us as well.

Throughout my life I've traveled in the wilderness. When I was younger, I wanted to cover as much ground, to traverse as much territory as I could. I didn't feel I'd really been anywhere unless I'd hiked or boated from Point A to Point B—from the headwaters of the river all the way down to its mouth; up the southern slopes, across the mountain divide, and down the other side. And the greater the distance between beginning and ending, the better.

Over the years I've come to appreciate the different quality of experience that comes from staying in one place for an extended time. Without dramatic changes in scenery it can seem at first that nothing much is happening. But in the course of hours and days we come to know where the sun rises and sets behind the mountains, how the light changes on the peaks, how the wind changes in the valley. We learn where the birds nest and sing on the tundra, when and where the animals come to drink at the river. The longer we stay in one place, the more closely we pay attention, the deeper and richer the layers of experience we discover.

Space is the distance we travel between here and there. The space we inhabit is *place*. Through patience and deep attention to where we are, we transform empty space into living place.

I want music to be like a place in the wilderness. Wilderness envelops us. It doesn't care whether we like it or not. It transcends us, utterly and impassively. We can get lost in wilderness. And as we lose ourselves, we can find ourselves. Wilderness has the power to take us beyond ourselves, to touch on what the Koyukon Athabascan people call Kk'adonts'idnee—the Distant Time—that older, forgotten world that still exists within us. Can we find this dimension of time in music?

As Henri Bergson observed, most musical time "has too many qualities, too much definition." In order to find a more fundamental time, he says "we should first have to obliterate the differences between the tones, then the distinctive characteristics of tone itself, retain of it only the continuation of that which precedes in that which follows, the uninterrupted transition, multiplicity without divisibility, and succession without separation."

Searching for this experience of time can lead us toward another dimension of music that extends beyond measurable space. Composers from Gabrieli to Ives and Henry Brant have embraced physical space as an integral element of their music. Composers from Ockeghem to Nancarrow have integrated multiple layers of tempo into the temporal space of their music. But is there a purely auditory space?

We hear sounds in measurable space. And in physical terms, sound is audible time. But we *perceive* sounds as something qualitatively different, less like objects and more like *forces*. This dynamic quality of sound creates its own kind of space and place.

Where the eye divides, the ear connects. Auditory space is a denser, more fluid medium than time and space as we usually experience them. In audible space, everything is connected, and the listener is always at the center.

From *The Immeasurable Space of Tones*

In visual space there's a phenomenon called ganzfeld. Immersed in pure color, the viewer loses all sense of distance and direction. I long for a similar experience in music. I want to find that timeless place where we listen without memory or expectation, lost in the immeasurable space of tones.

Composing Home (2004)

Like many of us here in Alaska, my wife and I have built our own house. More accurately I should say we *continue* to build our house.

It began three decades ago as a one-room cabin with a small loft. There was no running water and it was heated with a wood stove. After a few years the folks who built the cabin sledded it across the snow and dropped it onto a small foundation. Not long after that Cindy and I moved in with our teenage son, a large dog, and a small herd of cats.

After living through too many sub-Arctic winters in dark, cramped, and drafty cabins (without running water and sometimes without electricity), we craved light, warmth, and space. So we began the long process of transforming the cabin into more of a house. A crew of friends and I spent an entire summer raising the roof, expanding the loft, and adding large windows. This year we've continued the renovations, knocking out all the remaining interior walls and doors, adding a 12 × 12-foot atrium on two levels, installing an airtight fireplace, and replacing the old forced-air furnace with an in-floor hot water heating system. We've also replaced the old spiral staircase with a new set of "floating" (riser-less, stringer-less) stairs that we designed ourselves.

Before all this I had little interest in construction or mechanical things. Now I have a basic understanding of how our house is put together and how the water, heat, and lighting systems function. I also have a bit of hands-on construction experience. Not only has this given us a more comfortable home, It's also given me new a new set of metaphors and perspectives on my work as a composer.

Like homebuilding, composing music involves design, construction, and material. The most successful designs are usually the simplest. And the best construction is usually the most transparent. No matter how much good work may lie beneath the surface, technique should disappear, leaving only the beauty of the material visible or audible.

It's not quite a glass house. (This is Alaska, after all.) But from any point inside or out you can see right though our house. There are no rooms. Or rather there's a single twelve-hundred-square-foot room. Aside from closets, there are no interior walls or doors. The entire house is a continuous space on three levels. This design is a lot like the forms of my recent music, in which an entire composition is conceived as a single multi-dimensional sonority, transparent in form, harmony, texture and orchestration.

A small house enforces certain spatial disciplines. In our house there are few horizontal surfaces. Too often these become repositories for junk. If a house has lots of countertops, shelves, nooks, and tabletops, those places are likely to be filled with chotzkies, geegaws, and other useless objects. In a house with fewer horizontal surfaces one tends to keep only things that are truly useful or meaningful.

We also have relatively little furniture. A bench by the main entrance, a pair of easy chairs, a round glass dining table with four chairs, a small desk and chair, a platform bed, and a couple of dressers. There are no coffee tables, no end tables, and no floor lamps. All the lighting is either recessed or on tracks. There are no hanging fixtures. The idea is to minimize things and maximize space.

The temporal equivalents of things are events. In music I also favor vertical construction and empty space, minimizing events to maximize the moment. When not much is happening, then everything that does happen matters.

In both music and design, I want a sense of open space. Space is usually defined by line. And in designing our living space I've found myself following Kandinsky's geometry, from point and line to plane.

The highest ceiling in the house is in the living area, where the peak rises to sixteen feet. Since this side of the house faces nearby Ester Dome and the more distant peaks of the central Alaska Range, we decided to make the wall almost all glass. This raised a series of questions: How many windows would there be? What sizes and shapes? How close to the floor would the glass extend? How close to the ceiling? How close to the adjoining walls?

We lived with these questions for quite a while, sketching possibilities in notebooks and then on paper stapled to the wall. As we addressed each question we fixed points in space. When all the points were in place, we simply connected the dots.

In the loft the ceiling dropped precipitously from the center beam to the floor. The pitch was so steep that I could only stand upright in the center of the room. We knew we could gain about a hundred square feet of usable floor space if we raised the roof. The question was: How much?

We began by determining the ceiling height we wanted at the low end of the roof. Then we let the line rise from there, finding a height for the center beam that was both practical and pleasing. As we'd done in the living area, we let the shapes and sizes of our windows mirror the angles and dimensions of the space. This yielded two windows that contain no right angles. Oddly enough, these windows don't call attention to themselves. Instead they disappear, seeming more like transparent areas *of* the walls than holes *in* the walls.

In my recent music I've used similar means. The melodic lines rise continuously, and I let them follow their own contours. When a line approaches the upper reaches of its instrumental register, I simply let it drop down to the bottom and begin rising again. Since the ear is naturally drawn to the high points, the lower tones tend to disappear into the texture. The overall impression is that the lines are always rising. Points become lines. And the lines define the harmonies, the sounding planes of the musical space.

Like the birch and spruce forest around it, our house contains only a few basic materials. Selecting the materials for the vertical surfaces was easy. All the walls are sheetrock, painted white. All the windows and the exterior doors are made of high-efficiency glass.

Selecting the flooring wasn't as simple. Initially we considered wood for the kitchen and dining area, carpet for the living area, and stone for the hearth. But when we started mapping this out we realized we'd have an awkward intersection where three materials came together. So we decided to limit ourselves to one primary material on each floor: wood on the main floor and concrete downstairs.

Concrete is inexpensive, easy to maintain, and very effective for in-floor heating. We knew we wanted it for our downstairs bedroom and bath area. But we didn't want it to look like a grey garage slab. And although stained and acid-washed concrete has become very popular in residential construction, the more we looked at it the less we liked it. Most of what we saw looked like concrete trying to look like something else. We decided we wanted to let the concrete be itself. Since the downstairs is four feet below ground, we wanted the floor to reflect as much light as possible. So we settled on pure white concrete.

The mixture of cement, aggregate, structural additives, and water determines the strength and the overall appearance of concrete. The finishing method determines the texture of the surface. Instead of a machine finish, we chose a hand finish. The idea was to make things perfectly smooth with as little evidence of the mason's hand as possible. But perfection is impossible. And that's precisely the point. Ultimately every sweep of the trowel, every little gesture is visible. Those traces on the surface reveal the essential nature of the material and create the character of the finished floor.

After the concrete was poured, it was smoothed out level with a screed. Then we waited until the material had dried enough to be worked by hand. The first round of trowel work took a couple of hours. We took a break and then the mason went back to work on the finish coat. After a few minutes he turned to me and said: "We should leave it alone." His experienced hand and eye told him that the material didn't want to be worked any more, that we'd get the most beautiful finish by walking away and letting it cure.

I learned a lot about music from that mason, as I have from the carpenters, plumbers, electricians, painters, and other trades-people who have helped us build our home. The best of these workers don't force things. They don't call attention to them-selves. They simply reveal the essence of the designs and the char-acter of their materials. Their work must function. It must stand up with repeated use. Although they strive for perfection, they understand that perfection is rarely attainable and isn't neces-sarily the best solution.

At the completion of a task my carpenter friend John Murphy often says: "Perfect . . . But it'll do." This is ecological wisdom. Birch Pavelsky, another carpenter friend who is also a poet, puts it this way: "Wholeness is better than perfection." I'm still learning this lesson every day, in life and in art.

Birch says that his least favorite part of construction is foun-dation work. It's difficult, time-consuming, and not immediately gratifying. It's also the most important part of the job. If the foun-dation is off, even by a little, the entire structure will never be quite right. So he always takes his time and pays special attention to the foundation.

I try to do the same with my music. Often I spend as much

time sketching and preparing the foundation for a new piece as I do composing the finished tones and rhythms, the "piece" itself. Having gone though the process of excavation, laying the gravel pad and pipes for ventilation, pouring the slab and building the block wall for the addition to our house, I now understand the importance of foundation work in a much more physical way.

Renovations are notoriously expensive, and our home improvements have cost far more than we're ever likely to recover from selling the house. Still, it's worth it. After all, we live here. And though it's not exactly the house we'd build if we were starting from scratch, it's now tailor-made to fit who we are, where we are, and how we live. Our renovations have taken many months of my time. Instead of being in the studio composing, I've been digging holes, lifting beams, hanging insulation, hammering nails, and rolling paint. Yet I'm confident that eventually everything will go into the mix. It seems my work is all about composing home.

In the summer of 1947, an idealistic young man named John Haines left Washington, D.C., and headed for Alaska, looking for home. Sixty-eight miles from Fairbanks he reached a certain bluff high above the Tanana River. He knew his search was over. There he built a cabin with his own hands and found a life rooted deeply in the land. He also discovered a poet's voice that continues to resonate far beyond that particular place.

Almost fifty years later, John Haines left his life at the homestead for the last time. As we closed the gate, I turned to him and said: "This place will always be your home. But in another sense, your work is now your home."

For an artist maybe this is always true. Maybe art is the home we're always building for ourselves, somewhere between the stark truths of the world as it is and our longing for the world as we dream it.

Full Circle

One of a composer's fondest aspirations is that someone else will make the music theirs, giving the music a life of its own.

A few years ago, my friend Ari Vahan asked me to compose two songs on poems she had written in her native Gwich'in (Northern Athabascan) dialect. Although I don't speak Gwich'in, much of the text in my opera *Earth and the Great Weather* is in Gwich'in, so it's a language I've had in my ears for a long time now.

I asked Ari to record herself speaking the poems. Then I simply transcribed the melodies inherent in her speech. Ari used these songs at a youth camp to help teach Athabascan children a little of their ancestral language.

The following winter Ari traveled out to Bethel, in Yup'ik (Bering Sea Inuit) country. While she was there, she sang one of the songs. A woman who heard her asked Ari for permission to translate the text into Yup'ik and to sing the song at the Naming Ceremony for her daughter.

Not long after this Ari was in Anaktuvuk Pass, where someone asked for permission to sing the song in the local dialect of the Nunamiut, the Inuit people of the Brooks Range. Since then, the song has been shared with people in other villages throughout Alaska.

Over the years, I've learned and been given much from my Alaska Native friends and neighbors. So it's been profoundly gratifying to me that this little song has traveled full circle.

The Mathematics of
Resonant Bodies (2003)

I've always envied the hands-on relationship that painters and sculptors have with the materials of their art. The real substance of music always seems just beyond our reach. Still, music
is a tactile phenomenon. The musician touches the instrument,
and the sound passes through time and space to touch the drums
of our ears.

I've always loved percussion for its physical presence and for
the rich complexity of its sounds. More than any other family
of instruments, percussion embodies touch. As Steven Schick
observes, the essence of percussion is: "No instruments, only
sticks."

It's the element of touch that makes percussion specific. Different instruments played with the same sticks can sound like
a single instrument. And the same instrument played with different sticks can sound very different. Unlike pianos, clarinets,
and most other instruments, the sounds of individual drums,
cymbals, triangles, and gongs can vary greatly. When the percussionist travels, he may or may not carry his own instruments. But
he always carries his sticks. In a very real sense the sticks *are* the
instrument.

Our ears understand this. We rely on touch to identify sounds.
It's primarily the first few milliseconds of a sound (the "attack")
that we use to distinguish one timbre from another. But what
about the rest of the sound? If the attack gives a sound its name,
how do we hear its inner life?

Several years ago I composed *Strange and Sacred Noise*, a cycle for

From The Mathematics of Resonant Bodies

percussion quartet celebrating noise in music and in nature. One of the Noise pieces is scored for four tam-tams, playing waves of different periods that eventually crest together in an enormous tsunami of sound. When I first heard this piece (which was written for and premièred by the wonderful Percussion Group Cincinnati) I was startled. Amid the dense masses of broad-band noise I clearly heard voices, like a choir singing long, wordless tones. I called these "angel voices." And I wanted to hear them alone.

Working with a recording of the tam-tams, I filtered out most of the noise (in essence removing the sticks) until all that was left was that choir of angel voices. This became the point of departure for a new exploration of noise.

All noise contains pure tone. And the complex sonorities of percussion instruments conceal choirs of inner voices. In The Mathematics of Resonant Bodies my search has been to find and reveal those voices. I began this work by composing a new cycle of quartets. Steve Schick came to Alaska and recorded these pieces one part at a time. I assembled the recordings and then began filtering them as I'd previously done with the tam-tams. The result was a series of "auras" derived from the inner resonance of the instruments themselves. As the final step, I composed a series of solo parts to be performed within these sonic fields.

All the instruments in Resonant Bodies are noise instruments. They're also generic. Snare drums, tom-toms, bass drums, cymbals, and tam-tams are mainstays of Western percussion. And although each individual instrument sounds different, in a general sense they all sound alike. So it's the percussionist (with his sticks and his touch) who makes them specific, who gives them their particular names and profiles.

Like the listener, the soloist in these pieces is a solitary figure traversing enveloping landscapes of resonance.

Global Warming and Art (2003)

Some say the world will end by fire. Others say by ice. Here in Alaska, the land of snow and ice, we're beginning to feel the fire.

In the summer of 2000 the Iñupiaq community of Barrow—the farthest-north settlement on the mainland of North America— had its first thunderstorm in history. Tuna were sighted in the Arctic Ocean. No one had ever seen them this far north before.

The following winter Lake Illiamna on the Alaska Peninsula didn't freeze over. No one, not even the oldest Native elders, could remember this happening. In Fairbanks for the first time in memory the temperature never dropped to 40 below. Months of unseasonably warm temperatures, scant snowfall, and constantly changing winds were followed by an early spring. This was not the exhilarating explosion, the sudden violence of the sub-Arctic spring. It was the slow attrition of dripping eaves and rotting snow.

Once again this year, winter never really arrived. South central Alaska experienced a violent storm with the highest winds ever registered there. The Iditarod dogsled race had to be moved hundreds of miles north because there was not enough snow. Here in Fairbanks the mean temperature from September through February was the warmest on record. In November and again in February, we had freezing rain. At the small community of Salcha, the ice on the Tanana River broke free of the banks and jammed up, flooding nearby homes and roads. This is something that happens in April or May, not in the middle of winter.

Researchers have been predicting for years that the effects of global climate change will appear first and most dramatically near the Poles. From 1971 through 2000, the annual mean temperature in Alaska rose by 2.69 degrees Fahrenheit. (On a global scale, an increase of this magnitude would be cataclysmic.) Along with the volatile weather patterns of the past decade have come other warning signs. Glaciers are melting at increasing rates. The sea ice is retreating, disrupting subsistence whale hunting and bringing storm waves that are eroding the land out from under coastal villages. The spruce bark beetle is advancing north, the summer wildfire season is increasing in length and intensity, and the permafrost under the boreal forest is dissolving. Interior Alaska was once an inland ocean. It may become one again.

The weather is sick. The northern jet stream has drifted south, and southern weather has drifted north. Our neighbors—the moose, the white spruce, the boreal owl, the paper birch, and the snowshoe hare—know things we have long forgotten. Now it's time for us to wake up from the dream we've been living, time to remember.

In the North as in the South, we drive around in bigger and bigger vehicles on bigger and bigger highways, hoping that if we just keep moving fast enough it won't all catch up with us. But it's already here. The North has become the South. And as we're chattering on our cell phones, retrieving our voice-mail, zooming around town, or running to catch our next flight somewhere, the polar ice is melting.

What does global climate change mean for art? What is the value of art in a world on the verge of melting?

An Orkney Island fiddler once observed: "Art must be of use." By counterpoint, John Cage said: "Only what one person alone understands helps all of us."

Can they both be right?

Is art an esoteric luxury? Do the dreams and visions of art still matter?

An artist lives between two worlds—the world we inhabit and

The boreal forest. Photo by Dennis Keeley

the world we imagine. Like surgeons or social workers, carpenters or truck drivers, artists are both workers and citizens. As citizens, we can vote. We can write letters to our elected officials and to the editors of our newspapers. We can speak out. We can run for office. We can march in demonstrations. We can pray.

Ultimately though, the best thing artists can do is create art: to compose, to paint, to write, to dance, to sing. Art is our first obligation to ourselves and our children, to our communities and our world. Art is our work. An essential part of that work is to see new visions and to give voice to truths, both new and old.

Art is not self-indulgence. It is not an aesthetic or an intellectual pursuit. Art is a spiritual aspiration and discipline. It is an act of faith. In the midst of the darkness that seems to be descending all around us, art is a vital testament to the best qualities of the human spirit. As it has throughout history, art expresses our belief that there will be a future for humanity. It gives voice and substance to hope. Our courage for the present and our hope for the future lie in that place in the human spirit that finds solace and renewal in art.

Art embraces beauty. But beauty is not the object of art, it's merely a by-product. The object of art is truth. That which is true is that which is whole. In a time when human consciousness has become dangerously fragmented, art helps us recover wholeness. In a world devoted to material wealth, art connects us to the qualitative and the nonmaterial. In a world addicted to consumption and power, art celebrates emptiness and surrender. In a world accelerating to greater and greater speed, art reminds us of the timeless.

In the presence of war, terrorism, and looming environmental disaster, artists can no longer afford the facile games of postmodernist irony. We may choose to speak directly to world events or we may work at some distance removed from them. But whatever our subject, whatever our medium, artists must commit ourselves to the discipline of art with the depth of our being. To be worthy of a life's devotion, art must be our best gift to a troubled world. Art must matter.

We human animals have become an unprecedented force of nature. We're literally changing the climate of the Earth, threatening the entire biosphere—that miraculous network of connections that sustains all life on this planet, including ourselves. Ecosystems all over the world are in imminent danger of losing their wholeness and diversity, their capacity to sustain themselves. With ever-expanding global commerce, the same is true for diverse human cultures. If we hope to survive we have no choice but to expand our awareness, to recognize our interdependence and our obligations to all human cultures and to all forms of life with which we share this beautiful stone spinning in space.

Global warming is a disturbing manifestation of the inescapable truth that anything we do anywhere affects everything everywhere. If we choose to ignore this in our day-to-day lives, we may pay a terrible price on a planetary scale. The same is true for art and culture. Just as global climate change threatens the health of the biosphere, commercial monoculture threatens the integrity of the cultural sphere, from Greenland to Australia, from Papua New Guinea to Siberia.

Through the science of ecology, we've become increasingly aware of the rich diversity of species and ecosystems on the Earth. At the same time, with the advent of electronic media and instant communications, we've become increasingly aware of the rich diversity of human cultures on the Earth. We now understand that we need as many distinct plant and animal species as possible, living in whole, sustainable ecosystems. We also need the distinctive voices and visions of as many human cultures as possible.

Artists use the tools of perception and imagination to evoke the sound, the light, the *feeling* of our times and places. Art embodies creative thought. Creative thought is a fundamental part of our participation in creation. It's also essential to solving the problems of the world, from war and hunger to extinction and global warming. Amid the daunting realities of our time, the work of artists may prove to be more important than ever.

In the popular mythology Alaska is "the last frontier." But global warming signals the end of the frontier. Now even at the ends of the earth, even in the most remote wilderness, no place on this planet remains untouched by the actions of human beings.

Three decades ago I came to Alaska to "get away" from the world. But the world has followed me here in an inescapable way. I also came here to help save the wilderness. For years I worked as an environmental activist. When I left that work, I did so with the feeling that someone else could carry on my part in it, but that no one else could make my music. Implicit in this choice was my belief that in a different way, music could matter as much as activism. In recent years as the signs of climate change have become undeniable and as September 11, 2001, has changed the world, I've felt with increased urgency my responsibility to live up to this belief.

Today, as the horrors of war fill the news, I'm wondering again about the meaning of my life's work. In my current work I'm searching for musical equivalents of pure color, combining instrumental music with auras of computer-processed sounds. But how can I spend my time on such esoteric things? How can I make art that doesn't speak directly to world events?

Then I remember Claude Monet.

In 1914 the fabric of Western civilization seemed to be disintegrating. With the First World War raging, Monet was in his garden painting water lilies. His own son was in the war. The front advanced to within thirty-five miles of his home. Yet Monet continued to paint the reflections of clouds and willows in the waters of the pond at Giverny.

To a friend Monet confided that he felt "ashamed of thinking about little researches into form and color while so many suffer and die." Though he was old and in failing health, he might have found more immediate ways to express his concern about the state of the world. Instead, while young men died in combat within the borders of his own country, Monet painted water lilies. And the world is richer for his doing so. Those expansive panels of water, flowers, and mirrored sky were probably his greatest and most enduring gift to humanity.

Politics is fast. By definition it is public. Art is slow. And it often begins in solitude. In order to give our best gifts to the world artists must sometimes leave the world behind, at least for a little while.

It's a brilliant April morning. Sunlight shimmers on the snow. Last night in calm valleys the temperature touched on 20 below. With a renewed sense of hope and purpose, I return to work in my studio.

Photo by Dennis Keeley

Discography

(compiled by Sabine Feisst)

Clouds of Forgetting, Clouds of Unknowing (1991–95). Apollo
Chamber Orchestra, JoAnn Falletta (conductor). Norfolk,
Virginia. New World Records 80500. 1996.

Dark Wind (2001). Marty Walker (bass clarinet), Amy Knoles
(marimba and vibraphone), Bryan Pezzone (piano). Los
Angeles. Cold Blue Records CB009. 2002.

Dream in White on White (1992). Apollo Quartet and Strings,
JoAnn Falletta (conductor). Norfolk, Virginia. New Albion
Records NA 061. 1992.

Earth and the Great Weather: A Sonic Geography of the Arctic (1990–
93). James Nageak, Doreen Simmonds, Lincoln Tritt,
Adeline Peter Raboff, Dave Hunsaker (voices), Ron Lawrence
(viola), Michael Finckel (cello), Amy Knoles (percussion),
Robin Lorentz (violin, percussion), Robert Black (double
bass, percussion), John Luther Adams (percussion,
conductor). Fairbanks, Alaska. New World Records 80459.
1993.

The Far Country of Sleep (1988). Cabrillo Festival Orchestra, JoAnn
Falletta (conductor). Santa Cruz, California. New Albion
Records NA061. 1991.

The Farthest Place (2001) Amy Knoles (marimba, vibraphone),
Bryan Pezzone (piano), Robin Lorentz (violin), Barry Newton
(double bass). Los Angeles. Cold Blue Records CB0010.
2002.

Forest Without Leaves (1984). Arctic Chamber Orchestra and
Choir, Byron McGilvray (conductor). Fairbanks, Alaska. Owl
Recording 32. 1987.

The *Immeasurable Space of Tones* (2002). Marty Walker (contrabass clarinet), Amy Knoles (marimba, vibraphone), Bryan Pezzone (piano), Nathaniel Reichman (electronic keyboards), Robin Lorentz (violin), Barry Newton (double bass). Los Angeles. Cold Blue Records CB0010. 2002.

In the White Silence (1998). Oberlin Contemporary Music Ensemble, Tim Weiss (conductor). Oberlin, Ohio. New World Records 80600. 2003.

The Light That Fills the World (2001). Marty Walker (contrabass clarinet), Amy Knoles (marimba, vibraphone), Nathaniel Reichman (electronic keyboards), Robin Lorentz (violin), Barry Newton (double bass).Los Angeles. Cold Blue Records CB0010. 2002.

The Light That Fills the World (2001). Paul Dresher Ensemble, Paul Hanson (bassoon), Joel Davel (electronic mallet percussion), Gene Refkin (electronic mallet percussion), Marja Mutru (electronic keyboard), Paul Dresher (electronic keyboard), Karen Bentley (violin). San Francisco. *Musicworks* 82. Winter 2002.

Night Peace (1976). Atlanta Singers, Kevin Culver (conductor), Cheryl Bray (soprano), Joan Rubin (harp), John Luther Adams (percussion). Atlanta. Opus One Records 88. 1981.

Night Peace (1976). Cheryl Bray Lower (soprano), Nella Rigell (harp), Michael Cebulski (percussion), Atlanta Singers, Kevin Culver (conductor). Roswell, Georgia. New Albion Records NA061. 1992.

A Northern Suite (1979–81). Arctic Chamber Orchestra, Gordon Wright (conductor). Fairbanks, Alaska. Opus One Records 88. 1981.

songbirdsongs (1974–80). Armstrong Flute and Percussion Duo. Philadelphia. Centaur Records CRC 2273 ("Exotic Chamber Music"). 1995.

songbirdsongs (1974–80). Anne McFarland, Michel Cook (piccolos, ocarinas), Kevin Culver (percussion, ocarina), Tim

Emery, Scott Douglas, John Luther Adams (percussion).
Atlanta. Opus One Records 66. 1979.

Strange and Sacred Noise (1991–97). Percussion Group Cincinnati.
Cincinnati. In production.

The Mathematics of Resonant Bodies (2002–3) Steven Schick,
percussion. Fairbanks, Alaska.

RESOURCES
   www.johnlutheradams.com
   www.coldbluemusic.com
   www.newworldrecords.org
   www.newalbionrecords.com

Selected Bibliography

(compiled by Sabine Feisst)

WRITINGS BY JOHN LUTHER ADAMS

"Resonance of Place: Confessions of an Out-of-Town Composer," *North American Review*, January–February 1994, 8–18.

"From the Ground Up," *Utne Reader*, March–April 1995, 86.

"The Place Where You Go to Listen," *Terra Nova* 2/3 (1997), 15–16; repr. *North American Review*, March–April 1998, 35; repr. *The Book of Music and Nature* (Middletown: Wesleyan University Press, 2000), 181–82.

"Strange and Sacred Noise," *Yearbook of Soundscape Studies* 1, "Northern Soundscapes," ed. R. Murray Schafer and Helmi Järviluoma (1998), 143–46.

"Winter Music: A Composer's Journal," *Reflections on American Music* (New York: Pendragon, 2000), 31–48.

"Winter Music. A Composer's Journal," *Musicworks* 82 (February 2002); repr. *The Best Spiritual Writing 2002* (New York: Harper Collins, 2002).

"Global Warming and Art," *Musicworks* 86 (summer 2003); repr. *Orion* (September–October 2003).

INTERVIEWS

Mark Alburger, "A to Z: Interview with John Luther Adams," *21st Century Music* 7/1 (2000), 1–12.

Gayle Young, "Sonic Geography of the Arctic: An Interview with John Luther Adams," *Musicworks* 70 (1998), 38–43.

Liane Hansen, "Alaska Inspires New Soundscape from John Luther Adams," *Weekend Edition* (National Public Radio), February 12, 1995.

WRITINGS ABOUT JOHN LUTHER ADAMS

Eric Salzman, "Two John Adamses," *Stereo Review* 46/10 (1981), 140.

Thomas B. Harrison, "To Hear the Unheard," *Alaska Magazine,* February 1993, 96.

Kyle Gann, "Downtown Beats for the 1990s," *Contemporary Music Review* 10/1 (1994), 33–49.

———, *American Music in the Twentieth Century* (New York: Schirmer, 1997), 368–71.

Kyle Gann, "A Forest from the Seeds of Minimalism: An Essay on Postminimal and Totalist Music," Program Notes for the Minimalism Festival of the Berliner Gesellschaft für Neue Musik, 1998

Mitchell Morris, "Ecotopian Sound, or the Music of John Luther Adams and Strong Environmentalism," *Crosscurrents and Counterpoints: Offerings in Honor of Bengt Hambraeus at 70,* ed. P. F. Broman, N. A. Engebretnen, and B. Alphonce (Gothenburg: University of Sweden Press, 1998), 129–41.

Toshie Kakinuma, *Avant Music Guide* (Tokyo: Sakuhinsha, 1999), 238–39.

Joshua Kosman, "John Luther Adams," *New Grove Dictionary of Music and Musicians,* 2d edn, ed. Stanley Sadie and John Tyrell (London: Macmillan, 2000).

David Bündler, "Recent Works by John Luther Adams," *21st Century Music* 7/2 (2000), 14.

Phil England, "A Music Drama Celebrating Alaska's Arctic Refuge," *The Wire,* issue 199 (September 2000), 66.

Kyle Gann, "New Currents Coalesce: Since the Mid-1980s" in H. Wiley Hitchcock, *Music in the United States* (Upper Saddle River, N.J.: Prentice-Hall, 2000), 381–82.

Sabine Feisst, "Klanggeographie, Klanggeometrie: Der US-amerikanische Komponist John Luther Adams," *MusikTexte* 91 (November 2001), 4–14.

Kyle Gann, "American Composer: John Luther Adams," *Chamber Music* 19/1 (2002).

———, "Erasing the Lines: John Luther Adams Explores a New Landscape of Pure Harmony," *Village Voice*, June 18–24, 2003.

Allen Gimbel, "In the White Silence," *American Record Guide*, September–October 2003.

The quotations in the chapter "Resonance of Place" are drawn from the following sources:

Wendell Berry, *The Work of Local Culture* (Iowa City: Iowa Humanities Board, 1988).

Edmund Carpenter, *Eskimo Realities* (New York: Holt, Rinehart, and Winston, 1973).

Peter Garland, *Americas: Essays on American Music and Culture 1973–80* (Santa Fe: Soundings, 1983).

———, *In Search of Silvestre Revueltas: Essays, 1978–1990* (Santa Fe: Soundings, 1991).

John Haines, *The Owl in the Mask of the Dreamer: Collected Poems of John Haines* (St. Paul: Graywolf, 1993).

Knud Rasmussen, *The Intellectual History of the Iglulik Eskimo: Report of the Fifth Thule Expedition*, vol. 7 (Copenhagen: Gyldendalske, 1929).

R. Murray Schafer, *Music in the Cold* (Montreal: Radio Canada International, 1979).

———. *The Tuning of the World* (Philadelphia: University of Pennsylvania Press, 1980).

Paul Shepard, "If You Care about Nature, You Can't Go On Hating the Germans Like This," in *Deep Ecology*, ed. Michael Tobias (San Marcos, Calif.: Avant Books, 1988).

———. Thinking Animals: Animals in the Evolution of Human Intelligence (New York: Random House, 1978).

Catalog of Works

(compiled by Sabine Feisst; performance details
are for première)

Always Very Soft (1973), for double bass and three percussion
(Cal Arts Percussion Ensemble, Valencia, California, 1973),
withdrawn, 6:30.

Floating Petals (1973), for flute, violin, piano, harp, and
vibraphone (Cal Arts Chamber Players, Valencia, California,
1973), 6:30.

Prelude for Organ (1973) (G. Thomas Hazelton, San Jose,
California, 1973), withdrawn, 7:30.

The Sound Goes Round and Round (1974), for violin, viola, harp,
piano, cello, and other possible instruments (John Luther
Adams and Friends, Atlanta, 1974), withdrawn, variable
length.

Green Corn Dance (1974), for percussion sextet (Memphis State
Percussion Ensemble, Memphis, 1974), 7:30.

Night Peace (1976), for antiphonal choirs (SATB), soprano solo,
harp, and percussion (commission and première by Atlanta
Singers under Kevin Culver, Atlanta, 1977), 15:00.

songbirdsongs (1974–79), nine pieces for piccolos, percussion,
celesta, and ocarinas, with violin (optional) (John Luther
Adams and Friends, Atlanta, 1974), 50:00–60:00.

A Northern Suite (1979–81), orchestra suite in five movements
(commission and première by Arctic Chamber Orchestra
under Gordon Wright, Galena, Alaska, 1981), 20:00.

Strange Birds Passing (1983) (in memoriam Tadashi Miyashita),
for flute ensemble (Fairbanks Flute Choir, Fairbanks, Alaska,
1983), 6:30.

up into the silence (1978) (text by e. e. cummings), for medium
  voice and harp or piano (Cheryl Bray, Atlanta, 1978), 3:30.
up into the silence (1984) (text by e. e. cummings), arrangement
  for medium voice and orchestra (Lauren Pelon and Fairbanks
  Symphony Orchestra under Gordon Wright, Fairbanks,
  Alaska, 1984), 3:30.
Forest without Leaves (1982–84) (text by John Haines), for choir
  and orchestra (commission and première by Arctic Chamber
  Orchestra under Byron McGilvray, Fairbanks, Alaska, 1984),
  60:00.
Spring Rain (1985) (text by Chiyo Ni), for choir (SSAA) and piano
  (Atlanta Singers under Kevin Culver, Atlanta, 1985), 3:30.
In Search of the Long Line (1985), for piano (Thomas Dickinson,
  New York, 1985), withdrawn, 10:15.
In Search of the Long Line (1986), version for orchestra (Fairbanks
  Symphony Orchestra under Gordon Wright, Fairbanks,
  Alaska, 1986), withdrawn, 10:15.
Across Golden Distance (Fanfares and Antiphonies) (1986, revised
  1998), for brass and percussion (commission by Anchorage
  Opera, première by Air Force Band of the Pacific, Anchorage,
  Alaska, 1998), 9:00.
for Jim (rising) (1986), for four horns, 5:15.
The Far Country of Sleep (1988) (in memoriam Morton Feldman),
  for chamber orchestra (commission and première by Arctic
  Chamber Orchestra under John Luther Adams, Haines,
  Alaska, 1988), 15:45.
*Giving Birth to Thunder, Sleeping with His Daughter, Coyote Builds
  North America* (1986–90) (text by Barry Lopez), for clarinet
  (Eb and bass), violin, double bass, four percussion, and
  storyteller (commission and première by Perseverance
  Theater, Juneau, Alaska, 1987), 75:00.
Five Percussion Quartets from Coyote Builds North America (1990)
  (première by Amy Knoles and Paul Dresher Ensemble, San
  Francisco, 1993), 18:00.

Five Pieces from Coyote Builds North America (1990) (text by Barry
Lopez), for storyteller, E♭ and bass clarinets, violin, three
percussion, and double bass (Juilliard Focus Festival, New
York, 1996), 21:00.

Earth and the Great Weather: A Sonic Geography of the Arctic (1989),
for radio (commission by New American Radio, 1989),
withdrawn, 28:00.

Earth and the Great Weather: A Sonic Geography of the Arctic (1990–93)
(text by John Luther Adams), music theater for violin, viola,
cello, double bass, digital delay, percussion quartet, four
speaking voices, singers (SSAB), and recorded environmental
sounds (commission by Alaska Festival of Native Arts, 1991,
première by John Luther Adams and Company, Fairbanks,
Alaska, 1993), 75:00.

magic song for one who wishes to live and the dead who climb the sky
(1990), two songs for medium voice and piano (texts by the
Thule and Ammassalik Eskimo) (commission and première
by New Songs, Seattle, 1990), 5:00.

Five Yup'ik Dances (1991–94), for solo harp (Heidi Lehwalder,
Seattle, 1991), 12:00.

Strange and Sacred Noise (1991–97), six pieces for percussion
quartet (Percussion Group Cincinnati, Cincinnati, 1998),
75:00.

Dream in White on White (1992), for string quartet, solo harp or
piano, and string orchestra (Apollo Ensemble under JoAnn
Falletta, Norfolk, Virginia, 1992), 16:45.

Five Athabascan Dances (1992–96), for harp and percussion
(commission by U.S. Embassy in Tokyo, première by Just
Strings, Tokyo, 1996), 16:00.

Three Percussion Quartets from Earth and the Great Weather (1993)
(Percussion Group Cincinnati, Cincinnati, 1995), 28:00.

Crow and Weasel (1993–94) (story by Barry Lopez, script by Jim
Leonard Jr. and Barry Lopez), for piccolo and bass clarinet,
four percussion, celesta, harp, and string quintet

(commission by Children's Theater Company, Minneapolis, 1994), 90:00.

Clouds of Forgetting, Clouds of Unknowing (1991–95), for chamber orchestra (Apollo Ensemble under JoAnn Falletta, Norfolk, Virginia, 1996), 65:00.

Sauyatugvik: The Time of Drumming (1995), for orchestra (commission and première by Anchorage Symphony Orchestra under George Hanson, Anchorage, Alaska, 1996), 10:30.

Sauyatugvik: The Time of Drumming (1996), for two pianos, timpani, and four percussion (Shepherd School of Music Percussion Ensemble under Richard Brown, Houston, 1997), 10:30.

In the White Silence (1998), for string orchestra, celesta, harp, and two vibraphones (Oberlin Contemporary Music Ensemble under Tim Weiss, Oberlin, Ohio, 1998), 75:00.

Qilyaun (1998), for four bass drums or bass drum and digital delay (commission by Fairbanks Symphony Association, première by Scott Deal, Fairbanks, Alaska, 1998), 15:30.

Time Undisturbed (1999), for piccolo, flute, and alto flute (or three shakuhachis), three harps (or three kotos, or celesta, piano, and harp), cello, and sustaining keyboard (or sho) (commission by Kanagawa Cultural Council, première by Monophony Consort in Yokohama, 2000), 19:00.

The Light That Fills the World (1999, revised 2001), for amplified violin, double bass or contrabassoon, vibraphone, marimba, and sustaining keyboard (commission and premiere by Paul Dresher Ensemble, San Francisco, 1999), 13:00.

In A Treeless Place, Only Snow (1999), for harp, celesta, two vibraphones, and string quartet (commission and premiere by Third Angle New Music Ensemble, Eugene, Oregon, 1999), 18:00.

Make Prayers to the Raven (1996–2000), suite for flute, violin,

cello, percussion, and harp (or piano) (premiere by Min
Ensemble, Bergen, Norway, 2000), 16:30.

The Light That Fills the World (2000), for orchestra (Fairbanks
Symphony Orchestra under Gordon Wright, Healy, Alaska,
2000), 13:00.

Among Red Mountains (2001), for solo piano (Emily Manzo,
Oberlin, Ohio, 2001), 10:30.

After the Light (2001), for alto flute, vibraphone, and harp
(commission and premiere by CrossSound, Ketchikan, Sitka,
and Juneau, Alaska, 2001), 10:30.

Dark Wind (2001), for bass clarinet, vibraphone (or electronic
mallet instrument), marimba (or electronic mallet
instrument), and piano (commission by Marty Walker),
13:00.

The Farthest Place (2001–2), for violin, vibraphone (or electronic
mallet instrument), marimba (or electronic mallet
instrument), piano, and double bass, 11:00.

The Immeasurable Space of Tones (1998–2002), for violin,
vibraphone (or electronic mallet instrument), marimba (or
electronic mallet instrument), double bass or contrabassoon,
and sustaining keyboard, 30:00.

Red Arc/Blue Veil (2002), for piano, mallet percussion, and
processed sounds (commission and première by Ensemble
Sirius, Boston, 2002), 12:00.

The Mathematics of Resonant Bodies (2002–3), for solo percussion
and processed sounds (commission by Los Angeles County
Museum of Art, WNYC-FM, and SubTropics Festival,
premiere by Steven Schick, Los Angeles, 2003), 75:00.

Poem of the Forgotten (2004), for medium voice and piano (text by
John Haines), 5:00.

IN PROGRESS

The Place Where You Go to Listen, permanent sound installation for
the University of Alaska Museum, scheduled to open
December 2005.

Untitled work (in memory of Lou Harrison), for string quartet,
string ensemble, and two pianos.

Index

Page numbers in **bold** refer to illustrations.

Notes on the Compact Disc

The compact disc enclosed with this book contains three recent works that have not previously been recorded.

01 roar 10:46
for tam-tam and processed sounds
Steven Schick, tam-tam
Recorded by Scott Fraser
Charles W. Davis Concert Hall, University of Alaska Fairbanks
January 17, 2004
Produced by John Luther Adams and Nathaniel Reichman
Special thanks to Scott Deal

roar is one of eight pieces in *The Mathematics of Resonant Bodies*, a concert-length work composed for and dedicated to Steven Schick.

All noise contains pure tone. And the complex sonorities of percussion instruments conceal choirs of inner voices. In *Mathematics* my search is to find and reveal those voices. The soloist traverses fields of computer-processed sounds derived from the inherent resonances of the instruments themselves.

The Mathematics of Resonant Bodies was commissioned by the Los Angeles County Museum of Art, WNYC (New York), and the Subtropics Festival (Miami), with the generous funding of Meet the Composer.

02 *velocities crossing in phase-space* 9:41
for four drummers
Percussion Group Cincinnati
Allen Otte, James Culley, Russell Burge
with Stuart Gerber
Recorded by Paul Zinman
Patricia Corbett Theater, University of Cincinnati
November 13, 1998
Produced by John Luther Adams and Paul Zinman
Production Assistance by Nathaniel Reichman

velocities crossing in phase-space is drawn from *Strange and Sacred Noise*, a concert-length work celebrating turbulent phenomena in nature and noise as a gateway to ecstatic experience.

velocities crossing is a temporal canon of continuous acceleration and deceleration, in the proportions 7:5:3:1. Changes in velocity in the individual parts occur relative to a constant (and often unheard) pulse of quarter note equals 160. Complex relationships between the four parts occasionally converge in moments of coincidence.

Strange and Sacred Noise was composed for and in close collaboration with Percussion Group Cincinnati, to whom it is dedicated.

03 *Red Arc/Blue Veil*   12:26
for mallet percussion, piano and processed sounds
Ensemble Sirius
Stuart Gerber, vibraphone and crotales
Michael Fowler, piano
Recorded by Sam Griswold and Patricia Masterson
Center for Audio Recording Arts, Georgia State University
October 26, 2002
Produced by John Luther Adams and Nathaniel Reichman

Red Arc/Blue Veil is the first work in a projected cycle exploring the geometry of time and color. As in all of my recent music, I imagine the ensemble as a single instrument, and the entire piece as a single complex sonority. The computer-processed sounds are derived directly from the acoustical instruments.

Red Arc/Blue Veil was commissioned and premièred by Ensemble Sirius.

Total Time: 32:53
Special thanks to Jim Fox.